THE 50 COFFEE ADVENTURE

A fun, light and easy way ot build connections -
one magical conversation at a time!

Marc Winn

ISBN 978-1-910921-57-9

CONTENTS

50 Recipes for Achieving Coffee Mastery

The Coffee Grounds

The Coffee Filter

The Coffee Brewing

The Coffee Grinding

The Coffee Percolator

The Coffee Network

The Coffee Break

The Coffee Machine

Why take on the 50 Coffee Adventure?

Do you yearn for something different, but find it hard to shake off the old routine?
Do you sense there's something more, but don't know how to access it – yet?
Want to break existing patterns?
Are you up for a random, playful, breathtakingly simple adventure?

This adventure involves having informal conversations with people in informal locations. Invite people out for a coffee. That's it. You don't even need to drink coffee, if you don't like it, or you don't want to get wired. Take it easy. That's what it's all about.

Such a simple and seemingly pointless venture is bound to raise the eyebrows of some people around you.

The magic is that it defies logic. Logic says you have to work hard and deliver results: make things happen. This adventure is all about poking logic in the eye and challenging assumptions.

It's an adventure. Don't worry – there's no need to take out extra life insurance. But to be honest, there is a level of danger. Who knows what an adventure like this will do to the course of your life? What new direction will you follow, as a result of a few chats? If you're not careful, you could be selling your house, quitting your job, or even getting a divorce. So, take it easy; don't make too many rash decisions and enjoy what this adventure has to teach you about life.

You might not be whitewater rafting down the rapids or climbing Everest without oxygen, but this will still be a life-changing adventure – not just for you, but for everyone you meet. It even has the potential to benefit wider society. Change the world over coffee.

With something so easy, that delivers surprising, even world-changing, results – what's not to love?

Three reasons why you will love the 50 Coffee Adventure

It's not about the coffee. Although, I'll admit –   coffee is wonderful. It's about so much more – as you'll find out. It's about making connections and sharing your ideas – potentially to make the world a better place. Who knows what seeds you will sow, or beans you will grow, from a conversation over coffee?

1. It's breathtakingly simple and ridiculously fun

This is really a challenge to create momentum in your life, and to dismantle any unhelpful belief systems you have. You might even end up becoming a better person for it.

Break the patterns of day-to-day life with a challenge that's really simple to do – while potentially creating very unlikely outcomes.

Be playful. This challenge should feel mischievous and fun to do. Whether you want to break down your own barriers, enjoy yourself, meet interesting people, receive enlightenment, achieve your goals or give 'the system' a poke in the eye – this is for you. It's so simple, it's ridiculous.

2. You'll become a master of forming authentic human connections that create impact

This fun project helps you to develop a life skill that really matters. The ability to form and develop human relationships is something few of us are formally taught – yet, it's the foundation for all that's positive in the world. It's the basis of good health, great relationships and a fulfilling life.

This challenge not only teaches you how to develop authentic human connections, but to use those connections to help you to lead a meaningful life and make a difference.

3. You'll achieve more than you ever thought possible

Commonly, achievement is linked with productiveness and hard work. Most people focus on day-to-day effort, rather than understanding that year-to-year effectiveness is what really counts towards huge achievements. This challenge teaches you the value of cultivating connections, being brave enough to speak out loud, and giving yourself the time and space to reflect on the experiences you'll have.

It takes a lot less effort than you realise – to go places and make things happen.

Hopefully, by the end of this challenge, you'll understand – and believe – that you really can change the world, if you want to.

Simply one coffee at a time.

Why coffee?

For the purposes of this challenge, having 'coffee' is not necessarily literal. This is about spending around an hour with a person, informally, in any location, with any drink. Having virtual Skype or Zoom coffees is fine, too. And because it's so important, I'm going to capitalise the word coffee, and you are going to capitalise on these coffees.

So, why coffee at all? In short – because it's easy! Even a chronic procrastinator can do it. What if you want to change your world (or even the world) and all you have to do is take an hour a day, a week or a month, to hang out with someone over coffee?

Would it spark your interest to have a go? Could it break your current patterns? Can you make time to just be with someone instead of trying to do something? Will you join me on this adventure?

This is a breathtakingly simple approach to building momentum in your life without any hard work.

This exploration into the unknown doesn't require you to be an intrepid explorer – except into the human mind, and some fine coffee shops. There's no need to have a stuntman (or even a hard hat). You don't need to remortgage the house or sell the kids (although this might well cross your mind, as you go through the adventure...).

This startlingly simple challenge overturns your preconceptions about what it takes to make a difference to your life, and to the world around you.

It involves taking tiny steps – which anyone can do.

Our internal narratives often focus on the difficulties or the effort it takes to achieve things in the world. The truth is – a lot can be learnt and achieved from 'being', rather than 'doing'.

Most of us know how to be effective and efficient on a day-to-day basis. This challenge is about learning how to be effective and efficient on a year-by-year basis. And with the help of others, since one great proverb says: 'If you want to go fast, go alone. If you want to go far, go together'.

It's all about making connections, building relationships and seeing the impact over time. The quality, breadth and depth of individual relationships, whether in a company, community or family, are the foundation of any good life. If you want to create the right environment to progress, the quality and number of your relationships are key. And when you share your thoughts, hopes and dreams aloud with someone, you'll find that you are far closer to achieving them than you thought.

It's also about action – and solutions. The simple act of going for a coffee and consistently spending quality time with other human beings, is the very best way to

make things happen, over time. To be intentional about this process, both at individual and community levels, is to deliberately create the environment for good things to happen in the world.

It's quite possible that this 50 Coffee Adventure holds the keys to reinventing your life – and to solving any problem in the world. Big claim? We break it down… into coffee breaks...

The very worst that can happen is – you get to spend time with some interesting people, talking about interesting things. How much fun is that?

Consider these questions:

- How can you deliberately create the right foundation for your own individual success, and for the success of those you interact with?
- How can you nurture these coffee relationships?
- How can you develop your networks and the community, so that you all progress?

Try this experiment, and you might well discover that it's the solution you've been looking for.

How the 50 Coffee Adventure works

This is a simple five-step guide to maximising your results from the 50 Coffee Adventure. Follow the steps, and you'll be set for a profound learning experience with the capacity to change the direction of your life.

Step 1: Set yourself a bold, intuitive goal, by identifying your 'mission to change the world'.

Step 2: Go out and intentionally have 50 coffees – just to see what happens.

Step 3: Practise your skills – and over time, become a master of the art of having coffee.

Step 4: Develop a strong feedback loop, to maximise the learning experience.

Step 5: Maximise the impact, by being accountable and sharing the journey.

Don't worry if this list of steps blows your mind, like a super-powerful shot of strong coffee straight to the brain. This is the ristretto (the tiny, concentrated espresso) version.

All will become much clearer, once you see what's percolating in the rest of the book. (Also – don't worry – the coffee puns will soon run out…)

Step 1: Identify your mission to change the world

'My mission?' I hear you say. 'To change the world?' Yes – that's what I'm asking you to decide. This leap of faith might well be the most transformative part of the challenge. It can challenge your beliefs about what is possible in the world.

Although you can do the 50 Coffee Adventure without this step, and still find it valuable – the greatest long-term growth comes from taking this step.

You might believe that you've already found your mission, but it's important to check you're on the right path by asking one limitless question.

Before the challenge starts, ask yourself this bold question. And in answering, without even thinking, give the first intuitive response that comes into your head.

Imagine anything is possible. Instinctively – what one problem (in the world) would you want to solve?

Usually, the answer comes quickly – 'Eradicate Poverty!', 'Cure Cancer!', 'World Peace!' In some cases, your mind will try to argue with you, or contradict your initial response. It's important to go with your first, fast, intuitive answer, rather than the one your logical mind thinks up and tries to justify. It's not 'mission impossible' – it's 'mission is possible'.

You don't have to be the one to solve the problem yourself. The key thing about the 50 Coffee Adventure is to have a bold intention and a passion for seeing a problem solved. No outcomes are required. The key point is to **mention your 'mission'** in every conversation over coffee, at least once – just to see what happens.

Reflections

What did you learn about yourself, by asking this question?

Did you catch yourself trying to dismiss, or change, the initial answer? If so, what does this tell you about yourself?

If this revealed something new to you, how will this reflection change your life, going forward?

Do you believe you can contribute to solving this mission in the world? Explain.

Step 2: Have 50 coffees with intention

This part is simple. Go out and have 50 coffees, with 50 different people.

You can choose to set yourself a challenge like 50 coffees in 50 days, or take it easier and have 50 coffees in 50 weeks. Pick a pace that's both sustainable and enjoyable for you. Aim to coffee with new people, or ones you've never properly spoken to, one-on-one. Of course, you can still have a coffee with your friends, but see that as additional to the 50 Coffee Adventure.

Remember to mention your mission from 'Step 1' in every coffee – and try out some of the recipes from the next chapters in some or all of your coffees. The more intentional you are about this challenge, the more you'll get out of it.

Reflections

How often will you have coffee to make this challenge sustainable and enjoyable for you?
Once or twice a week

Which five people will you have your first five coffees with?

____

____

____

____

____

Step 3: Learn to become a master at having coffee

Think you can drink? In this book, you'll learn some techniques to make you a master at having coffee. 50 'recipes' have been created for you to try out, on your 50 Coffee Adventure. You don't actually need to use any of these recipes to complete the challenge, but I guarantee there will be something here to enhance your experience. How far you apply yourself to technical improvement is entirely up to you.

All the recipes are informed by learning from deliberate practice, over an extended length of time. Everything shared in this challenge has been tested over and over, in a live environment, and is proven to deliver results.

This book breaks down all the skills and techniques to enable you to achieve coffee mastery in a very short space of time. It is presented in bite-size sections (or spoonfuls), so you can try out individual skills in individual coffees.

The learning in these chapters is designed for you to progress from coffee amateur to coffee master. Anyone, at any level, will find this challenge accessible, and yet, mastering these techniques will put you in the top tier of people in the world who excel at connecting with others – all within 50 coffees.

Being world-class in connecting with other people has amazing benefits. It has the capacity to improve your health, your career and even your community.

Coffee mastery might give you an unfair advantage in life – although its potential is open to all, and is for the greater good. It demonstrates how to be intentional about your interactions with people, and how you can use these connections to transform your own life – and the world.

Reflections

Think about how well you connect with others, and summarise it, here:

What lessons have you learnt, that could improve the way you connect with others?

What skills would you like to improve or develop, to increase your power to connect with others?

What benefits have you found so far, in taking the time to connect with others?

Step 4: The learning an feeback loop

It would be too easy to just move from one coffee to another, and before you know it, they've all merged indistinguishably into one, like throwing every cup of coffee into a bucket, instead of savouring the unique flavour of each one. So, a great way to get more from your journey through coffee is to create some sort of feedback loop for yourself. A way of mulling over the conversation, taking stock and summarising your thinking, as a result of each coffee.

It's best to establish a method or system from the start, so that you can record and reflect on every encounter and learning point along the way. The act of writing and reflecting on all of this is as powerful as the journey itself.

So, how can you develop a feedback and reflection process that works for you?

If you want a ready-made template, use the specially-designed coffee reflection pages towards the end of this book to reflect on every coffee you have.

Or, as you prefer, you can write in a more free-form way – or, mind-map, blog, or vlog. Draw pictures, if you like. The method you choose doesn't matter, so please feel free to develop your own approach. The important thing is to develop some regular reflection time, to capture and feed back on your experience.

Ask yourself questions like:
- What did I learn from the experience of having coffee with that person?
- How has it changed the way I see the world?
- How will it change the way I move forward?

The more you reflect and feed back to yourself and the world, the more value you create from each of your interactions.

Find a way to make the most of your learning from the experiences, and you will accelerate the progress you are making.

Reflections

How am I going to reflect on this journey to get maximum learning from the experience?

Which other areas of my life could use a more regular reflective practice?

Step 5: Be accountable and share the journey

This step ensures that you give yourself the best chance of completing the challenge. You're much more likely to complete the mission if you've told other people that you're going on this adventure. Share the steps and let them hold you to account.

Here are some suggestions to give you more public accountability, to help you complete this challenge:

- Get a group of friends to do the challenge with you.
- Post videos or messages on social media to share your learnings. Remember to use the #50coffees hashtag, if you do.
- Write a blog or video diary.
- Have a group of friends go on the adventure with you.

Share the steps of your journey, as far as possible. Just announcing your intention at the beginning might not be enough to keep you going. And it won't create the maximum benefit for those around you, either.

Sharing your journey will inspire others to take a similar journey – and it also makes it easier for you to get your next coffees. Meet with someone who reaches out to you because they've seen your message and they're interested in talking to you. Or receive recommendations for fascinating coffee-mates from readers, subscribers or viewers.

The best way to learn is to teach. Share what you're learning, along the way.

Ultimately, find an approach that works for you, to demonstrate your accountability, and to share and spread what you've learnt.

Reflections

How will you make yourself accountable for completing the 50 Coffee Adventure?

How are you going to inspire others and have impact on them, as you take this journey?

50

Recipes for Achieving Coffee Mastery

The Coffee Grounds

1. Your own style

One of the most important lessons in life is: what works for one person might not work for you. Take the lessons from these recipes, try things out, but never forget who you really are. The magic truly happens when you take influences from the outside world and add what is quintessentially you to the mix: your own personal brand and your own secret sauce.

Celebrate your individuality rather than hide it. If you're funny, add humour to the framework you develop for connecting with the world. If you are quirky, develop quirky approaches to how you 'do coffee'.

The more you add 'you' to the process, the more you will connect with people who like you for who you really are. This is living authentically.

It's always useful to step outside your comfort zone and try new things to see what happens. But if something doesn't 'sit right' with you, or feels uncomfortable – if any of these conversational approaches don't sound like you – feel free to adjust them to suit you and the person you're meeting.

Be authentic. Being someone you're not – especially whilst building relationships – is a ticket to a lonely life. Most powerfully, understand who you are, and accept and celebrate this. Then, you can bring that real essence and magic of you to all your interactions.

Like life, much of this challenge requires you to be comfortable in your own skin. This isn't always easy to achieve, but it is such an important thing to do. In the long term, it is impossible to achieve happiness without being true to yourself. That's why it is important to try these approaches, continue those that resonate – and be prepared to develop your own way of doing things. Do coffee your way, in your own style.

Ingredients
Yourself.
These recipes and approaches.
Your own style.

Method
1. Combine all ingredients.
2. Enjoy.

Reflections

Who are you really?

____

____

____

How would you describe your personal style?

____

____

____

How can you bring more of you into every human interaction?

Where, in your life, are you not being yourself, right now?

----

2. No agenda

You don't need an excuse to spend time with someone, or a reason to reach out and have coffee with another person. Aim to meet people, just because it's good to connect with another human being. coffee with no strings.

The best conversations often come when there is no agenda; no need for an outcome. Just meet for the love of spending time with someone else – and see what happens naturally, through connection.

That isn't to say that an agenda is a bad thing. But consider meeting people just because you want to, rather than because you need to. It's refreshing for both of you. The only objective you have is to mention – just once – how you would like to change the world. Then, see how the conversation develops. Other than that, there is zero agenda or expectation of any outcome.

You will be amazed by the outcomes that unexpectedly come into your life when you spend time with people just 'because'. Broach the subject of your 'mission' – your wish to change something in the world – and see how much further you can go. Maybe your coffee-mate will simply listen while you formulate your ideas, or will help you or challenge you, or connect you to someone else who moves you closer to your mission. Or maybe your conversation will go elsewhere. Who knows? If you're not tied to a specific

outcome – anything can happen. The main aim is to simply connect with another person, enriching your experience and ability to build relationships. Anything else is a bonus.

Try intuitively reaching out to people you just want to spend some time with. Enjoy what happens.

Ingredients

One person you want to talk to.

Method

1. Arrange coffee with chosen person.
2. Remove agenda – except to mention your global wish or mission for change!
3. Go with the flow.
4. See what happens.

Reflections

How often do you spend time with people, just for the sake of it?

____

____

____

What do you want to change in the world, and how will you slip it into conversation?

____

____

____

What good things might happen, during, or as a result of this coffee?

3. How to ask for coffee

If the person knows you even slightly, it's usually easy to invite them for coffee: 'Hey, X. I would love to catch up for coffee sometime. Let me know a time and place that would work for you. Y.'

No explanation. Providing no reason or information is more intriguing than explaining why you want to meet. The human mind tends to fill information gaps, so a simple, short request makes it easy for people to respond.

However, if the person doesn't know you at all, expect your success rate to fall slightly if you employ that phrasing or method.

The trick to increasing your success rate is to keep it short and sweet, and also mention an area of commonality. Refer to a mutual connection: a person or subject of interest, your shared community or perhaps a simple, shared love of going for coffee!

'Hey A, I was with B the other day and your name came up in conversation about (subject) C. I would love to have coffee with you, because I think we would have a fun conversation. Let me know a time and place that is good for you. D.'

Or: 'Hey X, I see we have a shared interest in Y. I would love to catch up for coffee some day to have a chat about this. Let me know a time and place that is good for you. Z.'

Tailor it to suit the way you talk, also considering the individual and whatever their needs might be. There's so much information about people publicly available – a little research into your common ground and their time and location pressures will increase your success rate. Remember that you want to meet people's human side, rather than their formal, professional side. Meeting people about shared personal interests/passions is much more effective than meeting to discuss work issues.

There is an art to asking. The more you test out methods and learn what works for you and for other people, the better you will get.

Ingredients

Someone for coffee.
A line to invite them.

Method

1. Select someone you want to meet.
2. Find something or someone in common, to use as an introduction. Or if they know you, skip this and simply ask them to coffee.
3. Invite them for coffee, using simple lines that suit their needs and your style.
4. Meet.

Reflections

What would motivate you to meet a stranger for coffee?

Which individuals would you like to meet for coffee, and what common ground do you have?

What line will you use to invite your next coffee-mate?

4. Where to meet for coffee

Where can you have a good coffee? (In the capitalised meaning of the word, although a good coffee to drink is brilliant, too).

Location, location, location. Don't let the lack of a perfect meeting place be a barrier to connection. At the end of the day, any meeting is better than not meeting at all. But because the surroundings have an effect on the nature of the conversation and the connection you develop, choose wisely when you can. The objective of a coffee is to deepen connection, so arrange to meet the other person in a place where you're both able to relax and be yourselves.

Formal locations create formal conversations. Informal locations create informal conversations. True connection develops in the informal realm. So, get comfortable with your coffee-mate in surroundings conducive to talk and build closer connections.

There is a Danish cultural phenomenon – 'hygge' (pronounced "heu-gah") – associated with comfortable, friendly social gatherings and intimate get-togethers with family and friends. A website devoted to this defines it as: 'The art of building sanctuary and community, of inviting closeness and paying attention to what makes us feel open-hearted and alive. To create well-being, connection and warmth. A feeling of belonging to the moment and to each other. Celebrating the everyday'. It is a dedication to simplicity and appreciation, to giving and receiving. Try to arrange meetings in places with 'hygge'. Cosy coffee shops or intimate surroundings are good places to meet people to have conversations.

The setting has a big influence on what happens in a conversation – so it's important to make your default meeting locations conducive to developing intimacy, comfort and openness. Virtual coffees on Skype or Zoom allow you to have intimate conversations from the comfort of your own home, with people you might never have considered possible to reach. You can even enjoy a coffee on the phone!

Get out into the world, which now includes the vast virtual world at your fingertips, and make those closer connections over coffee with people in your choice of place and space.

50 coffees in beautiful, intimate spaces will make a much greater impact on your life than 50 coffees in stiff, formal meeting rooms or sterile surroundings.

Ingredients

A cosy place for coffee (your default meeting place), or;
Several options to research or consider.

Method

1. Consider your requirements for comfort and cosiness.
2. If you are meeting out of your area, research online, or accept recommendations.
3. Invite the person for coffee in your chosen or agreed place.
4. Have coffee.

Reflections

What's your favourite place for coffee, and why?

____

____

____

What makes a good environment or atmosphere for conversation?

____

____

____

The Coffee Filter

5. Hug people hello

Shaking hands is one type of greeting that most people are comfortable with. Others, like me, prefer to hug it out. No matter what the situation, try to start every coffee with a hug instead of a handshake. Whenever you meet someone – even if they put out their hand – open your arms, with a big smile on your face and say, 'I'm a hugger'. The majority of people feel obliged to go in for the hug.

Starting every conversation with a hug is a deliberate move to make the conversation intimate and informal. It suggests a mutual vulnerability that subtly shifts a conversation to a deeper level of connection – even before it begins. It's the simplest thing you can do to shift people's regular patterns of conversation to another level.

Do respect anyone's wishes not to hug, however. Don't take any rejection personally: some people have issues in their past that makes hugging problematic for them. You might even feel resistant to doing this yourself; but challenge yourself – when you confront your own fears and make yourself vulnerable, great things can happen. Aim for a 90% success rate, because everyone forgets sometimes and goes back to old, hardwired patterns of formality!

It's not just a friendly act – there's an awful lot of scientific research on the power of hugging. According to a study by psychologist Sheldon Cohen, published in December 2014, hugging even helps to cure common cold symptoms. Cohen says, "… if stress puts you at risk for disease, then having high levels of social support seems to protect people from that risk."

Other research has found that a hug instantly reduces the stress hormone, cortisol, in our bodies. Instead, the body releases oxytocin – the 'trust hormone' – during a hug. Oxytocin reduces blood pressure, lowers anxiety, relieves stress, and improves memory.

If you hug hello with the next 10 people you meet, a new richness will emerge in your life and you'll experience the birthing of a whole new type of conversation. Hugging could even save your life!

Changing the world doesn't have to be hard. Transformation can come from a simple action in your life. Here, it is initiated in how you greet someone. This simple act sets the tone for what follows.

If every handshake became a hug, the world would be a very different place. Try it – and see how your world changes.

Ingredients

Two arms (or equivalent).
One smile.
Vulnerability.

Method

1. Upon first meeting someone, smile and open arms.
2. Move forward, welcomingly.
3. Before touching, if you meet resistance (expressed by facial expression), say, 'I'm a hugger'.
4. If they don't respond affirmatively, respect their personal space.
5. If they consent, hug closely.
6. Talk, with added connection.

Reflections

How do you feel about greeting someone you don't really know – with a hug?

What will it take to overcome any resistance to hugging:
a) in yourself?

b) in the person you're meeting?

What positive things will a hug give you?

6. Merging

Have you ever felt such a deep connection to someone that you know what they're thinking? Research from cognitive scientists (Columbia University and Dartmouth College) showed that close friends have remarkably similar wiring in their brains. You might guess that's because friends grow to be alike, over years. But what if that happens almost instantaneously? Science has discovered that the brainwaves of two complete strangers having a conversation start to match one another! A research study, published in Scientific Reports by the Basque Center on Cognition, Brain and Language (bcbl,) concluded that 'neural synchrony' develops when two people have a conversation: their brain-wave rhythms synchronise, effectively connecting both of their brains to work together towards the shared goal of communication. Just having a conversation causes people's brains to start to work in synch, simultaneously! Who knew? Well, scientists apparently – but now we do, too.

Think of the implications of this knowledge. It's not too great a stretch for us to develop further technology for communication: telepathy. It's not all woo-woo. Many people know what it feels like to communicate with someone in that way, even momentarily. You can often pick up on the 'vibes' of someone who's angry, sad, happy or in love, without them speaking – and without even seeing their facial expression. And face-to-face, you might look into someone's eyes and feel a connection that creates an indescribable depth of knowing and understanding. Something even beyond empathy.

Developing and extending these fleeting moments of profound communication can offer a richness of interaction with the world, beyond words.

What if we were to use our minds, as well as our mouths, to make a deep connection? If conversation allows our brain-wave rhythms to merge – what more might go unsaid? How much can be communicated by other nonverbal means – even through your thoughts alone? Synchronise brainwaves. Merge your thoughts with someone else. See what happens.

Ingredients

Two brains.

Method

1. Start a conversation.
2. Feel the connection.
3. Communicate non-verbally – even telepathically – for seconds at a time.
4. Enjoy closer connection.

Reflections

Think of times when you have felt that telepathic connection with someone. Who was it? What were the circumstances? How did it feel?

____

____

____

How can you can bring this into everyday meetings and conversations?

____

____

____

7. Active listening

This is the number one skill in the discipline of having coffee for impact. Many of us believe we're listening to the person talking to us when, in fact, we're mostly listening to the voice inside our head.

If you're thinking 'What voice inside my head?' – that's the voice I mean.

We often pay much more attention to our own thoughts than to what the other person is saying. Or we feel the need to fill any gaps with words of our own. It's not all about you and your opinions. A better approach is to actually listen to the person, without attachment or judgement. Listen and learn. You can reflect on the conversation later, in your own time.

Listening doesn't mean passively allowing the person to talk, while all you hear is 'yada-yada-yada' – it takes effort and action on your part to listen well.

Some guidance for active listening:

- Really concentrate on exactly what the speaker is saying. 'Listen' rather than just passively 'hear' the words.
- Be truly present in the moment – not drifting into your own thoughts and memories, or planning what you should say next.
- Listen with all your senses. Eye contact, facial expression, body language and tone of voice can convey messages, too.
- A pause isn't just a chance to chime in with your own opinions, questions or comments. A silence isn't inherently 'awkward' – even if you feel awkward about it. Get over yourself. Use silent moments for reflection, to absorb information and assimilate it. And to give the speaker a chance to add anything more. Sometimes that clear breathing space allows the unexpected to occur.

For active listening, use:

- Smiling, eye contact, posture, mirroring
- Focus, without distraction
- Positive reinforcement – nods and encouragement
- Remembering and questioning
- Reflection, clarification and summarising

If this is all new to you, it might feel strange – as breaking any lifelong habit does; but do make these changes. You're worth it. You have 50 coffees to practise a skill that will utterly transform your life and the way you interact with the world.

The more you listen, the more you'll notice, and the more magic will occur.

Ingredients

Another person.
An open mind.
Concentration.
Patience.

Method

1. Encourage the other person to speak.
2. Listen actively – carefully and encouragingly.
3. Ask questions or clarify, as appropriate.
4. Check your understanding.
5. Leave to brew, and enjoy.

Reflections

Think of your last conversation. What percentage of the time did you spend listening? And how much was spent speaking?

____

____

____

Remember a time when you felt that someone was really listening to you. What did they do or say, to make you feel this?

____

____

____

8. Leading with vulnerability

Brené Brown's Power of Vulnerability is amongst the most-watched TED talks of all time. It's certainly one of the most influential bodies of research on human interaction that I've encountered.

Dr. Brené Brown is a research professor at the University of Houston who has spent well over a decade studying courage, vulnerability, shame, and empathy. One significant finding of her research is that vulnerability is the key to human connection.

We put on a front. We 'big ourselves up'. In our day jobs, many of us spend our whole lives selling ourselves – promoting our skills, experience and achievements. This is often at the cost of our own health, a deeper understanding of others and greater benefits to all. Instead, we must develop relationships with people first, and trust that good things will come out of good connections.

'I'm a very private person!' – you might cry. But at what cost? How does that label or belief isolate you and shut you off from making deeper connections? You might be horrified at the prospect of showing your vulnerabilities. This might be one of the greatest challenges for you – but it's one that can transform your approach to every conversation. It can even transform you – and your life.

If you hide your own vulnerability, you shut down the opportunity to connect with another human being. If you only share the light and not the darkness, the possibilities to maximise your connection fall away.

If someone asks, 'How are you?' most people say: 'Fine!' and move quickly on. But to connect more deeply in a conversation, take your guard down. Simply have the humility and honesty to say, in a balanced way, how life really is for you.

This doesn't mean confessing you're a train wreck, or rambling on for hours about your woes, or even your loves. No need to spill your guts or expose yourself completely. Not on a first date, anyway. Provide an honest, brief appraisal of how you actually feel, deep down, at that moment. Choose to express your hopes, dreams or fears. Let someone truly see you, from the start, without your armour on and your barriers up. There's no greater bravery.

Being vulnerable early on in a conversation is a great way to build trust. It also creates space for the other person to put their shield down and show something of themselves, too.

In every interaction, try to lead with vulnerability. It can feel terrifying to give of yourself with vulnerability at first, but the more you do it in every conversation, the more it opens unimaginable doors in life.

The objective of every coffee meeting is not to show how great you are. The objective of every coffee is to connect as deeply as you can with another human being.

Life becomes so much richer, and your relationships begin to blossom in ways they never have before.

Ingredients

One other person.
A whole bunch of vulnerability.

Method

1. Be vulnerable.
2. Connect with a deeper bond.
3. Reap the benefits.

Reflections

How are you – really?

Which vulnerabilities are you comfortable to share?

9. Ask great questions

Are you a quiz master? Interrogator? Chat-show host? Teacher? Torturer? Curious child? Investigator? Hopefully, you're more subtle than these, in conversation – asking great questions in your own inimitable style.

But what is a great question? Rather than following the normal patterns of conversation, which skate on the surface, a great question gets beneath that – reaching unseen depths.

Something like 'What do you do?' is not a great question, because it's one we're used to, and we are conditioned to answer it with a well-rehearsed, brief, standard phrase. A question like that doesn't get people out of their usual patterns – and therefore, it doesn't deepen your connection with them. Ask something less expected. Asking 'why' a person does something is more provocative than 'what' they do. Although a question like 'what makes you happy?' is good, too.

Ask questions that get people to stop and really think, and you create the right environment for a richer conversation.

Great questions have the power to make people truly think, reflect on their answer, and even learn something about themselves – as well as teaching you a lot about them.

At the end of this book, there's a section with 50 Great Questions to Ask In a coffee. But before you take the easy route and flip the pages to see, think of some searching questions yourself and note them below.

Ingredients
One enquiring mind.
A spoonful of great questions.

Method
1. Have coffee.
2. Drop in one great question.
3. Don't stir, until you have an answer.
4. Repeat.

Reflections

What great questions could you ask someone, that they've never been asked?

Choose one great question. What answer would you give?

----

10. Meeting people where they are

- How well do you connect with people who are not 'like you'?
- What is there to talk about, when you have little in common?

We're used to having conversations with people we know, and who are like us – we're all more comfortable in our echo chambers of like-mindedness, to some degree. It's harder having conversations with people from a different world to ours. Taking a journey to new places just gives you new challenges to expand your learning.

I see life as a 7-billion-person jigsaw puzzle. There are all sorts of pieces waiting to be put together. Every single person has something to teach you. Everyone has at least one piece of information, knowledge or learning to offer you. Your job, in a conversation, is to find that piece.

Individual human's necessities are very different – you only have to look at Maslow's hierarchy of needs. One person's desire for self-actualisation (e.g. achieving spiritual enlightenment or changing the world) might be hard to hear for a person who's struggling to secure the basics of existence, like food and shelter. In coffee conversations, understand that different individuals can be in very different places from each other.

Meet your coffee-mate where they are at. Understand their world view, without judgement. Achieving your own expectations, or having a desire for certain outcomes, are not the point of the conversation. Your job is just to connect with another human being.

Overwhelmingly, people just want to be heard and accepted for who they are; so there is little for you to do, other than listen. People tend to like people for how well they listen, rather than what they say.

If the person is reticent to speak, or if you don't know what to say to get them talking, just ask a question that shows you're interested in them.

The magnificence of a conversation is magnified by your service to another human being: in simply being there and asking questions. Meeting whatever they say with curiosity and interest is a key to connecting with people.

During the conversation, think:

- How can I provide the space for this person to come alive?
- If I were them, in their world, what questions would allow me to fly?

For reflection after the conversation, ask yourself:

- What was this conversation trying to teach me?
- Which part of the human puzzle was this?

Ingredients

One person, completely different from you.
Open mind.
Pertinent questions.

Method

1. Remove all judgement or pre-conceptions.
2. Remove any expectations or outcomes.
3. Ask questions that show you are interested in the other person.
4. Seek only to connect.
5. Appreciate their perspective.
6. Afterwards, reflect on your learning.

Reflections

Think of the person you want to meet for coffee. Imagine you are in their shoes, living their lives. What's it like? How does that feel?

What questions can you ask to discover what's important to them?

____

____

____

11. The line

The objective of this exercise is to develop deep personal relationships with people, but the world is largely a realm of formal, impersonal relationships. Many people are just not used to informal interactions – so, they may not feel safe when people behave informally with them. The same goes for intimacy or 'personal' conversations. Where do they draw the line? Where will you draw the line? Will you be crossing the line? Will I ever stop talking about lines?

Understand that some people may not be ready for the types of conversations you want to have. You will probably sense an energetic line they're resistant to crossing. You'll soon learn to recognise other people's boundaries. There may be taboo subjects or levels of intimacy they resist – at least until more trust is built. Recognise how they signal their discomfort – whether through reticence, monosyllabic answers, facial expressions or body language – and don't push them beyond their comfort zone, either in terms of the questions you ask them, or in the personal information you give them.

Open-heartedness and deep connection only develop in an environment of trust and safety. You might want to be completely open with your experiences and information, but be sensitive to the other person's comfort zone: only be as open as the other person is ready for you to be. The more you push someone who is locking down, the more they will lock down.

You being super open when the other person has shut down (or in their eyes, you 'oversharing' or discussing taboos) defeats the object of the exercise, which is to build connection. It will put them off, and create division, if you cross their line. It becomes a one-way conversation, rather than a deepening, two-way, closer connection.

To get some people to open up, patience, subtlety and gentleness are required. In order to create the comfort zone for mutual connection, foster trust by observing the line they draw. Stay within it, until they know you better and allow you in. Read the signs.

Ingredients
Openness.
Sensitivity.

Method
1. Be open, but sensitive to the other person's responses.
2. Don't push the conversation in directions they don't want to go .
3. Foster trust, in the present, and for the future.

Reflections

Understand that your own taboos are not other people's. Which lines are you unwilling to cross? What subjects do you not want to discuss?

How have you recognised 'the line' in other people?

12. Boundaries (and no boundaries)

To maintain good balance in life, during coffees, understand where your boundaries are. Although I've suggested that you make yourself a little vulnerable, you're certainly not obliged to make yourself a complete walkover. There might be boundaries you don't want to cross, in terms of talking about certain areas of your life, or certain

subjects (like sex or football); or there may be things you cannot or will not do – such as making promises or commitments you're unable to fulfill.

If you find yourself taking on too much or agreeing to things you can't deliver, you're clearly struggling to maintain your boundaries.

Have a deeper understanding of where you will and will not go, in conversation. If you let people overwhelm you, or push you to places you don't want to go, you need clearer, firmer boundaries.

Understand where your edges are, and look to develop strategies and frameworks that help you to maintain balance. Reinforce these boundaries during conversations, to maintain stability in your life and to protect yourself.

There is, however, a downside to maintaining strong boundaries. It takes energy and effort to do it. And the more tired, stressed, unwell, or cognitively overloaded you are, the more challenging and harder it is to maintain your boundaries. In those instances, you might be swayed into things you don't want to do or can't do, simply because it's easier to be swept along and concede, rather than stand your ground.

Another way takes a lot less energy. And that's to have a strong, unwavering sense of who you are. Some people have this strength of identity from the outset; for others, this develops over time, as their confidence increases. It might be developed through years of personal development, reading, workshops, therapies and self-reflection.

The more grounded and sure you are in your identity and sense of self, the less energy you need to maintain your boundaries. Self-assuredness can be effortless and limitless – with roots so strong that boundaries are hardly an issue.

People who know themselves and wholly accept themselves don't need to put energy into maintaining boundaries. Their sense of security and stability means that they naturally don't move from their position – it's who they are. They know where they stand. They say no when they want, or need to. They're confident, self-assured and never a push-over, so they hardly have to think about strategies to defend or protect themselves against others' persuasion, through obligation or deference. They don't just do it. They know who they are, and can simply be themselves.

Creating firm boundaries, fighting to keep them and hiding behind them offer only a temporary solution. What is truly needed is deep self-acceptance.

Ingredients
Boundaries; or,
A strong, unwavering sense of who you are.

Method

1. Use the first ingredient, as necessary, until you develop the second.
2. Then, use the second, and simply be.

Reflections

Recall a time when someone 'crossed' your boundaries. How did that feel?

How will you assert your boundaries in future? What will you say, and how?

What work will you do (or what have you done) to develop a greater sense of self?

13. Free from attachment

This theme features in many of these recipes, but it's good to make it very clear. In your coffee or interaction, the more attached you are to a planned outcome, the more you narrow down the wider opportunities. Remember how you feel when things don't 'go to plan'? Here's an easy way to avoid that, during this challenge. Have no plan. At least, not for any particular result or 'product' of your coffee with someone.

Having an intention for a conversation is fine. But when you are attached to a specific outcome, other opportunities can be missed.

And another thing, if something your coffee-mate says evokes strong reactions or responses in you, this comes from your particular expectation of the individual, rather than you just being present for them. The more you feel any resistance to what they're saying, the more you unconsciously want to control the conversation. Relax. Wake up and smell the coffee. You might discover even better outcomes if you simply allow all possibilities to arise naturally, rather than 'controlling' the conversation and steering it in a preconceived direction.

The ideal approach is 'engaged indifference'. This means having an intention for the conversation and being genuinely interested – but not having an expectation or needing an outcome from it.

It's not just for coffee. You can apply this way of being to your whole life, to great effect.

Many people start a conversation from the perspective of what they want to get out of it. But wanting something from a meeting, or a person, can be a barrier to connection. The objective of a coffee is to develop a relationship and connect with the other person.

Many people have an expectation of individuals (either consciously or subconsciously). They expect them to act in a certain way, say a certain thing, or give them something they want. This attitude, also, is a barrier to connection.

A great practice is to clear your mind of the need for outcomes and expectations, and trust that everything is exactly as it should be. Everything that comes up in conversation is of interest, and all that happens is meant to be.

Allow conversations to flow wherever they go. The less you try to control them, the more the eventual outcomes will surprise you. Anything can happen, if you let it.

Ingredients
An intention.
No expectations.
No outcomes.

Method
1. Have an intention for the conversation in mind, but don't let it rule you.
2. Listen, talk and connect.
3. Recognise any strong reactions as simply residual attachment to outcomes or a need to control.
4. Give up control and let the conversation flow.
5. Stay clear-minded and open to all possibilities.

Reflections

What sorts of expectations do you have of people?

____

____

____

How will it feel to talk to someone – and have NO expectations? No outcome?

____

____

____

The Coffee Brewing

14. How can I serve?

How can I serve? This is a great question to ask yourself, especially when in the presence of another human being. You don't have to be a barista to do it.

Your 'service' could mean offering someone kind words, encouragement or saying something nice. It could mean asking the person what their challenges are and connecting them up with solutions. It could be about sharing contacts or sharing information. Remember that listening in itself is one of the greatest acts of service.

Living in the service of others is an extraordinary way to live life, and one that will bring you much greater happiness. Try it and see.

- Do find a way to serve without self-sacrifice. Depleting your own reserves is not a sustainable way to make a difference.
- Do not serve to satisfy your own 'need to be needed'. That's more about you, than about the other individual.

Serve freely. It's incredibly liberating. The magic occurs when you come from a place of unconditional service: doing it because you expect nothing and need nothing in return. Seeing the other person's delight, satisfaction, relief or comfort fills you up, as well as them – and in that respect, you need nothing more. If that sounds crazy and too philanthropic for words – give it a go. I guarantee you'll feel great, knowing that you've done some good to others.

To feel this mutual benefit, serve in a way that brings both of you energy. To live your life with humility through serving others is highly transformative for all concerned. Try it out for yourself. And for others!

Ingredients
A desire to serve the other person.
A way to do it.

Method
1. Go into your coffee, thinking: 'How can I serve?'
2. Listen.
3. Think, 'How can I serve to bring us both energy?'
4. Act on it, and serve them.
5. Enjoy.

Reflections

Recall a time when you gave someone help, advice or service. What happened? How did that feel?

____

____

____

List the kinds of things you might offer someone, as an act of service to them.

____

____

____

15. Celebrate the bright spots

It's often easy to focus on the negative. Our human brains are just wired that way, as an evolutionary throwback from our ancient past – when we needed to be constantly alert to danger, to prevent us from harm by predators.

Most of us don't need to beware of violent wild animal attacks at any moment. Least of all in a local coffee shop. Unless we haven't paid. Although we have naturally evolved since those primitive stone-age days, positivity can still require deliberate cultivation. We need some tricks and tools to help us to see the positives in life.

When you're speaking to a person, an effective way of creating connection is to celebrate the bright spots – the positives you see in them. If you feel, hear or see something good about the person, take the time to tell them.

Whether it's their great sense of humour, their sensitivity, their upbeat outlook, their genuine smile, their astuteness or their ability to tell a story – look for the good and positive in them, and tell them what you see (or hear). Tell them what's good about them. You might think they'll know it already, but people's self-perception is often

much less positive than we presume.

Appreciate them, and share it aloud. This is a really good practice to develop, because searching for the good in every human being helps you to like them (even when you don't, initially) and most importantly, it helps you to connect more deeply with them.

Take time to celebrate the bright spots of whoever you're with. And while you're at it, take time to celebrate your own.

Ingredients
Awareness.
Focus on positives.

Method
1. Search and filter for positives and good things ('bright spots') in each person.
2. Include yourself.
3. Live life accordingly.

Reflections

Think of the last conversation or meeting you had with someone. What are that person's 'bright spots'?

____

____

____

List your own bright spots. Compliment yourself!

____

____

____

16. Tell me your story

We all like stories. A lot can happen between 'Once upon a time' and 'The end'. In fact, anything can happen. However, we don't often get a chance to fill in the blanks ourselves. "What do you do?" is the first question people typically ask someone they've just met. But their answer doesn't usually give you a clue about who a person really is. To connect deeply with someone, rather than knowing 'what' they do – it's more important to understand 'why' they do it.

To start a deeper conversation with someone new, ask an open question like: 'Tell me your story.' Yes, you might see raised eyebrows for a second, but it's worth it. They can take your request however they like – and talk about family, life-story, career, passions, motivations. Anything is possible – it's their choice. People aren't often asked to put their lives into context, so asking a question like this is usually empowering and enlightening for both of you. The few minutes in which a person describes their own story can be powerful and informative. There are so many ways to find out more about people – so, the important thing is to develop your own style. Find questions and ways that work for you; but in principle – get under the surface of what people usually ask.

We are all programmed to follow patterns – especially in conversation. You know when you ask someone an apparently open question: 'How are you?' that the stock, superficial answer will be 'Fine.' But ask them to tell you about their health and wellbeing, or their hopes or motivations, and you will learn far more, at a far deeper level.

Gently disrupting standard patterns gets people to stop and think; so ask a question that surprises them and requires them to give a considered response. If you make people think more, you immediately create a deeper connection. When you transform a day-to-day 'what do you do?' question into something far more meaningful, it tells a person you are interested (and interesting) – and their response tells you much more about them. Who knows? You might all live happily ever after. The end.

Ingredients
An interesting question or invitation to talk.
Active listening and encouraging responses.

Method
1. Invite the person to talk, in a way that gets beneath the surface.
2. Avoid using standard patterns and stock answers.
3. Make them think.
4. Listen and explore.

Reflections

If someone said, 'Tell me your story' – what would you say?

Write down 3 'deep' questions to tell you something interesting about a person.

17. What challenges do you have?

One simple question that reveals a lot is 'What challenges do you have?' In conversation, someone answering this question reveals a great deal about them, and what they're facing. You might be able to assist them in meeting their challenges, if you can. But that isn't the main purpose of this exercise. The real power lies in simply providing the space to allow people to articulate the challenges they're facing.

Their responses are often very revealing. Where you find shared challenges (which happens often), you have an opportunity for greater connection and mutual support on the journey.

Getting to know the challenges people face (and, indeed, sharing your own challenges) is a simple and constructive way of deepening a relationship. Solutions often occur through discussion, and in describing a challenge, the speaker will often identify how to find a way through, for themselves.

There's an old saying, that 'a problem shared is a problem halved'. Be the person who halves problems. Get twice as much out of each coffee.

Ingredients
One question.
Shared experience.

Method
1.   Ask: 'What challenges do you have?'
2.   Listen.
3.   Share.

Reflections

What challenges do you have?

____

____

____

What further questions might help you to find a solution?

____

____

____

18. Blank sheet thinking

In conversation with people, you might find that people are stuck, or are struggling in life. You want to help – right? Leave your coffee-mate in a better state than you found them, I say.

Certainly, you don't want to get into counselling or coaching them. Leave that to the professionals. It's just coffee. But there is a simple exercise you can do with them: a blank sheet thinking exercise. Anyone can use this to create a powerful and challenging conversation. Even over coffee. It goes like this. You say:

- If you had a chance to design your life, from scratch – would you build it this way again?
- What aspects of your life would you change, and why?
- If you started again from a blank sheet, how would you build your life?

This type of questioning approach is great for encouraging breakthrough thinking. We often don't see the solutions to our own challenges because we can't see beyond where we are today.

This process doesn't mean they have to completely blow their life up (although to be honest, they do, sometimes!). What you're offering them is some space to explore beyond their current realms of perceived possibility. And this can be really valuable. Follow up this exercise by asking something like:

- How do you get 80% of the way there, without changing too much?

This helps to bring it back to the present, without it being too unsettling for people. No need to go all the way, on a first date. coffee and a blank sheet is plenty.

It's remarkable how often this exercise creates some form of breakthrough for the person. A momentary, hypothetical, separation from their current reality allows new solutions and possibilities to arise – almost instantaneously.

You can also use this exercise on yourself, to deal with any blockages that occur for you, in or out of your coffee journey.

Ingredients
A blank sheet of paper – even a hypothetical one.
Questions.

Method
1. Start from a blank sheet.
2. Ask questions.
3. Build a life.

Reflections

If you had a chance to design your life from scratch – would you build it this way again? What aspects of your life would you change, and why?

____

____

____

If you started again from a blank sheet, how would you build your life?

____

____

____

How do you get 80% of the way there, without changing too much?

____

____

____

19. And then what?

One of my favourite questions to ask over coffee is: 'And then what?' And I don't mean just desserts. Or even another coffee – or coffee. I mean, after people tell me things – their hopes, their dreams, their story, their challenges, their goals, their mission.

'And then what?' I keep asking that question until it can go no further. 'When you eventually retire, or when the kids leave home, or when you've got that promotion, or sold that business – then, what?'

To help people to identify their plan for life, I ask that question as many times as it takes, to help them to get closer to their own truth and recognise their most important values.

Helping people to confront the end of their life is also useful in this process; to distill what really matters. I ask:

- What would your epitaph be? What will be your legacy? What will people say about you at your funeral? Moreover, how do you want your days to be, and what kind of life do you want to look back on?
- And then what?
- What will it all get for you?

Ask such questions and you usually end up with something intangible like 'contentment' or 'peace', rather than material goods. Whether your ultimate answer is happiness, love, family or good health, this process serves as a guide to how life could be lived today, rather than how you might live life in the future. Start now.

Most people want very simple things in life, in the end. And yet, most people lead quite complex lives in the present.

Why wait till the end? You could get those simple pleasures now. This is the realisation you and your coffee-mate can come to, over a coffee. What's most important, at the end of the day?

Just like travelling to any destination, you need to know where you're going before you plan the journey. Ask: where will life take you? And then, what?

Before you set out to do something, it is really important to know the ending you want. And if you can, start living that end result – today.

Ingredients

One question: And then what?

Variation:

Extra questions for looking back at the end of your life: What would your epitaph be? What will be your legacy?

Or about your life purpose: What's the point of that? What will it get for you?

Method

1. If someone is telling you about their hopes, dreams, aims, actions or future, ask: 'And then, what?'
2. When they answer, repeat 'And then, what?' until they can't answer, or until enlightenment or bewilderment occurs.
3. Variation: ask additional questions as above.
4. NB: You can ask yourself the same questions.
5. Absorb the learning, and live life accordingly.

Reflections

What would your epitaph be?

____

____

____

What do you want to leave as your legacy?

What will it take, to start living the life you want to look back on, with pride?

And then, what?

The Coffee Grinding

20. What if it was easy?

Ask yourself – and others – this question: What if it was easy? This is the greatest question to ask, to create better solutions and easier paths for people. Think about things that were difficult until an easier way was found: like drinking water before plumbing and glasses existed. Or going for a coffee without these recipes. We live in a time in which every challenge humanity faces has been solved – or is about to be solved. During this technological and information revolution, difficult problems become simple ones, as a result of innovation.

There's always an easier way. It might simply require a shift in mentality. No matter how tough a situation, or how hard a problem, there is always a way for it to feel easier. There's even instant coffee, if you don't have time for a real coffee.

What if it was easy? Give yourself the gift of asking that question – and you'll find a way. Ask that question, and more often than not, your mind will work more creatively to come back with the answers. Try asking someone else that over coffee, too.

If you want an easier life (or if you want other people to have easier lives), be the person who asks that question – a lot.

Ingredients
One question.

Method
1.   Ask: 'What if it was easy?'
2.   Let your mind open to possibilities.
3.   If asking another person, invite them to open their mind to solutions.

Reflections

Think of a challenge you have – and answer the question 'What if it was easy?'

What could happen? What possibilities are there?

____

____

____

How do you feel, now?

____

____

____

21. Self compassion

Do you treat yourself well? Do you consider yourself with kindness and compassion? Or are you self-critical and hard on yourself? Sometimes we are our own worst enemy, since negative or critical self-talk can be a blight on our lives – and on others'.

Consider how you feel about giving yourself continuous positive regard. And if that thought makes you uncomfortable – it's a signal that you have work to do. Because how can you be the best version of yourself, and how can you offer help and service to others, if you treat yourself unkindly?

Sometimes, our own lack of self-worth can leak out in ways that hurt others – through sarcasm or negativity. Do we really want to hurt our loved ones, our friends and colleagues, through our own lack of self-compassion? Your judgement plays a role in any conversation – and any negative self-judgement will be as clear and unattractive as wearing a label across your forehead. So, notice if you are being self-critical or judgemental about who you are, or what you say or do. Simple techniques can be applied to make life far easier:

- Notice any negativity, but detach yourself from it by saying to yourself, 'That's interesting. I appear to be giving myself a hard time.' This separates and distances you from the emotion.

- Stop those thoughts in their tracks and replace them with words of kindness.
- Or, stay so fully in the present moment – mindfully – with your coffee-mate, that there is no time or space for negative thoughts or worries. There is only now. Choose to be compassionate now.

Practise compassion towards other people you meet. And most of all, apply it to yourself.

Ingredients
Compassion.

Method
Apply compassion to self and others.

Reflections

Consider any negative thoughts you have about yourself, or any critical self-talk you have. Whereabouts in your body do you hear or feel these?

Take a few moments to visualise this next step, with your eyes closed (after reading it). Imagine turning down the volume of any critical voice until you can't hear it. Take those bad feelings out of your body and float them far away (or shoot them out like a cannonball!). Fill the space they leave with love. How does that feel?

Think of kind words to tell yourself.

---

22. Surfacing tension

Sometimes a conversation can make us feel uncomfortable. Even with friends, let alone strangers, they may say something that evokes a strong response in us. There are often two responses to this – one internal, one external:

1. The 'pretend it isn't happening' method, which involves holding onto any tension you feel, without telling the other person about it. This feels awkward, builds resentment, and can leave an individual brooding for some time afterwards about what they could, or should, have said – even berating themselves for not expressing what they thought at the time.

2. The blunt, challenging reaction – 'How dare you say that!' This response is more about fighting what's been said and who's said it. This often causes escalations of negativity within the conversation, that break down a relationship. The opposite of what you want.

Neither of those approaches is helpful. However, there is another way that, when mastered, provides more positive outcomes and allows things to be said.

3. Make a statement like 'For some reason, what you've said is creating an angry/ frustrated/negative response in me'. This detaches the statement from the speaker, and the emotions from yourself, without blame or upset.

Your response should always come from you as the 'observer of the emotion' rather than the 'experiencer of the emotion'. It provides a more objective response and this way, you can both approach the emotion with curiosity, rather than conflict. It allows you to discuss what is happening without apportioning any blame.

This technique will allow you to have far braver and edgier conversations and help you to feel much stronger inside. It is of great benefit to those you are speaking with, too, because it allows them to experience what you're feeling without having to defend themselves too strongly.

Ingredients
Contentiousness.
Emotion.

Method
1. Unexpectedly have a conversation that makes you uncomfortable.
2. Notice what you're feeling.
3. Observe aloud, something like: 'For some reason, what you just said has brought up a feeling of …… in me. Isn't that curious?'
4. Talk it through.
5. Move on.

Reflections

What kind of conversations, or people, evoke negative emotions, for you?

What sort of phrase might you use to express how you feel, with detachment and curiosity?

What will the effect be?

23. What is the barrier to love?

This is a really good question to ask yourself – or to ask the person you are with: What is the barrier to love? We all struggle with other people, at times. On occasion, this coffee challenge might bring you together with someone you find difficult. It will also bring you in contact with other people, who are themselves struggling.

One technique to address this struggle is to imagine the person as the young baby they once were, innocent and vulnerable. Then, just imagine what awful story might have unfolded, for them to turn out the way they are now. What hurt or rejection they must have experienced, that led them to protect themselves with such anger (or whatever unappealing behaviour they display now, that you're finding difficult). How sad that is, for them! Imagine this, and compassion and love usually follow quite quickly. It doesn't matter that you made up the story and filled in the blanks. It changes how you feel about them, and helps to break down the struggle between you – that's all that matters. Even feeling pity for them changes the dynamic, so you can feel more accepting of them – which is one step closer to love than before.

It is possible to love anyone – and everyone. With some people, there are barriers in the way – yours or theirs. Notice them. Ask yourself what the barrier is, to loving them or to them loving you. What is the barrier to love? Consider how those barriers can be removed, in order to improve your relationship with that person – and take action. Find a way that works for you, for the other person, or for the situation.

It may not always be possible for you to entirely remove your barrier, or help someone else to remove a barrier, with this question. That's OK. However, asking it will definitely help you to remove some barriers, or at least start to dismantle them. This can only be a good thing for you, for them, and for the world.

Ingredients
A person you're finding difficult.
One specific question: What is the barrier to love?

Method
1. Recognise that you're struggling with someone.
2. Ask the question: What is the barrier to love?
3. Answer it.
4. Find a way to remove it, get around it, or get over it.
5. Do it.

Reflections

Is there someone you find difficult? What is it about them that's hard to deal with?

What might have happened in their life, to make them this way?

How do you feel towards them, now?

24. The mirror

A great piece of advice is: "Whenever you are triggered, look in the mirror." That is, to identify the reasons why you react badly or unhelpfully on occasion, you should take a good look at yourself. Take responsibility for how you feel. Some people can't look themselves in the eye or hate to reflect on themselves and see all their blemishes. They'd rather hide them. But resistance to self-reflection can burn you like acid. It eats away at you, unless you do, finally, reflect on yourself – and surrender to the gift of the new reality you can create.

In the Buddhist tradition, there are five hindrances (or triggers) affecting our minds. These triggers are universal: we all experience them, and they hinder our ability to see clearly or concentrate on our direction in life. The five hindrances are:

1. Sensory desire: the particular type of wanting that seeks happiness through the five senses of sight, sound, smell, taste and physical feeling.
2. Ill-will: all kinds of thoughts related to wanting to reject, or feelings of hostility, resentment, hatred and bitterness.
3. Sloth and torpor: heaviness of body and dullness of mind that drag one down into disabling inertia and thick depression.
4. Restlessness and worry: the inability to calm the mind.
5. Doubt: lack of conviction or trust.

Over coffee, observe your conversations carefully, and you might recognise any of these being triggered within you. Sometimes, our reaction is extreme and disproportionate to a person's behaviour, which might be minor or trivial – but it triggers old 'stuff' in us from our past (childhood bullying, schoolteachers, parents). Reflect on yourself and your reactions. Maybe there's something about the person today that makes you feel awful. When you think about it, it's because they remind you of a nasty teacher you had, when you were six, and scared of the Daleks on TV, and you'd hide behind the sofa to feel safe. If only you could do that now! Understand that some of your responses were learned in childhood, as coping strategies – and they aren't necessarily appropriate, these days. You can't hide behind the sofa any more – not even metaphorically. You need new, adult ways to respond.

The real magic starts when you become aware of these responses, recognise them and identify why you are responding that way. Once you appreciate this, you can detach from that old emotion and choose to react differently.

'That person is arrogant/appalling/crazy/stupid' or: 'they said an arrogant appalling/crazy/stupid thing' are responses from the external perspective. You blame someone or something outside yourself for your own negative feelings.

The internal perspective would say: 'that person triggered an angry response in me – what has it touched in me, and how can I address this?' or 'them saying x triggered an angry response in me – why am I doing this to myself, and what can I do differently?' In this case. you take responsibility for your own feelings, and for how you react.

When you understand that you are in control of how you respond, you start to gain control of your life. Every trigger becomes a gift: it's the stimulus for a mini-research exercise into the origin of the wound that created this response in you. And from here

on, with that knowledge, you can choose to respond differently.

A Viktor Frankl quote sums it up: "Between stimulus and response there is a space. In that space is our power to choose our response. In our response lies our growth and our freedom."

Notice what 'sets you off' reacting badly – and instead of blaming the person you're talking to, look to yourself or your past, for the reason why. Recognise that you are responsible for your own feelings. And in future, take control, and react differently.

Capture the occasions when you experience any one of the 5 hindrances and think about the 'why' behind them. Build a process like this, and your worst conversations will become some of your best conversations – because of the learning they give you. They create a deeper understanding of yourself, and the recognition that you can take control and choose to behave in a different way.

The more you let go of blaming others and the less you're affected by triggers, the more you can meet every conversation, and every person, from a place of deep connectedness.

Ingredients

An appreciation of stimulus-response.
One to five triggers or hindrances.
A metaphorical mirror.
Time to reflect.

Method

1. Have a conversation with someone.
2. Recognise any uncomfortable feelings.
3. Recognise the triggers.
4. Explore within yourself why you respond in this way.
5. Recognise old patterns of behaviour and past events that caused this.
6. Recognise that you no longer need to behave in that way.
7. Take control and respond differently.
8. Change and move forward.

Reflections

When was the last time you were triggered, and by whom?

____

____

____

Can you identify why you might have responded in this way?

____

____

____

How will you respond differently next time?

____

____

____

25. Look back a year

People often say they feel stuck, or that nothing's changing in their lives. Same old same old. This is mainly their perception from day to day, or week by week. They can't see that anything is different from the day before, or last week.

'What's been happening?' you might ask. 'Nothing,' they reckon.

One of the best ways to break this cycle is to ask the person to 'look back a year' – and see what their life was like, then.

A lot can happen in a year. Even more can happen in a decade. Shifting the timespan

by which you assess your progress can profoundly change your perception and experience of how well you're travelling in life.

If you ever feel that you're making no progress, look as far back as you need, to feel great about how far you have come. It just takes a moment to do, and then frustration or negativity turns into self-compassion – or another positive feeling.

While travelling on this 50-coffee journey, if you feel that you're making little or no progress, look back on how your life was, before you started this adventure. See the changes that have happened in your life and in your perception, since you began this journey.

It feels impossible to perceive change on a moment by moment basis, but it is very easy to see it over longer time spans. If you, or someone you are with, is stuck – look back a year. See how that shift in perception holds the key to getting things moving again.

Ingredients

One stuck or despondent person.
One invitation: 'Look back a year'.
Memories.

Method

1. Look back a year.
2. Remember how life was, a year ago.
3. Observe what's different now.
4. Notice how far you've come.

Reflections

Look back to this time, a year ago. How is life different?

____

____

____

____

Look back five years – or ten years – how far have you come?

26. Keep going

Maybe you've had a few coffees, but you start to think, '50 seems an awful lot!' After the initial excitement of coffee is over, doubts can creep in: What's the point? Where is it going to take me? Why am I doing it? Should I be doing something more useful? Shall I drink tea?

These are normal feelings and responses to making unconditional connections. We have come to expect to 'get' something for our efforts – often immediately. The mind wants to focus on the outcomes we have been taught to believe in – 'focus on a target, take action, achieve it'. 'Concrete outcomes equal concrete results', they say. So, maybe this all feels counterintuitive. You start wondering if maybe you should give up, and instead, knit a scarf, or run a marathon, or become a millionaire? Something practical, with an end product you can see.

So, maybe you've hit a wall. However, keep going. Trust the process. The desired outcome is simply to increase human connection – it's a focus on the process, rather than the results. One way to help is to reframe any doubts. Therefore, ask yourself:

- Have the coffees brought me new relationships? Deepened existing relationships?
- How do those relationships make me feel?
- Have I enjoyed spending time with people?
- If something wasn't tied into outcomes like success, money etc. – would I still do it?

This process challenges you to consider how you travel through the world. It shakes the old order of your life – and even challenges your old values. It's quite normal for your old self to resist, in some way.

'Keep going' sends a signal to your old self that you want something more valuable in life than what you have been told to value by society, by work, by business books.

Surrendering to the process of getting to 50 coffees, no matter what, gives you sufficient time to reprogramme your beliefs about how the world works. Stopping at 10 or 20 coffees only allows these old programmes to stay in place. We want a seismic shift to take place. So carry on. Keep going.

Surrender to the process. Be aware of the loudness of the old-self's voice in its attempts to keep you where you are. Resist. You will receive unimaginable rewards if you only continue.

You will be amazed by what happens when you truly prioritise human connection, above all.

Ingredients

50 coffees.
Persistence.
Resilience.

Method

1. Keep going.
2. If doubts creep in, keep going.

Reflections

How are you feeling about the Coffee Adventure, so far?

____

____

____

What good might come from completing the adventure?

____

____

____

The Coffee Percolator

27. Just breathe

Breathing is such a vital thing – and yet we take it for granted. It sounds strange, but breathing properly is the simplest thing you can do to make the biggest difference. Most people tend to breathe with shallow, short breaths that don't fully oxygenate them – and in stressful circumstances, this can lead to hyperventilation. Conversely, fully inflating our lungs by taking in deep, long breaths of cleansing oxygen feeds our blood and organs; while breathing out long exhalations removes poisonous carbon dioxide and other waste.

If you are breathing properly, you should be able to feel your ribcage rise and fall as you rest your hands just above your belly. It doesn't matter what size your belly is, it's what's inside that counts – what's inside your ribcage, not your belly, that is. Make it natural – no exertion, strain, or force – just use longer, deeper, careful breathing that fills and empties your lungs completely.

Simply put – slow and deep is the way. Because breathing is an unconscious act, we forget we're doing it. Yet, drawing our attention to it and bringing our consciousness to our breathing means we can take control of this vital life-giving function.

Notice your breathing, take control, and see what happens. Try it out, in real life.

- How does a conversation change, for you, when you take the time to breathe well during it?
- What if you started or finished a coffee with a few deep, slow breaths?
- How does this breathing method affect you in the rest of your life, beyond the coffee?

This is a simple, yet transformative experiment for you to take into the rest of your life.

Ingredients
Air.
Conscious attention.

Method
1. Bring your consciousness to your breathing.
2. Take in a deep, slow breath.
3. Breathe out, deeply and slowly.
4. Repeat, for the rest of your life.

Reflections

Close your eyes and breathe deeply for a few minutes, consciously. What effects do you notice?

In which situations would you find this breathing helpful?

---

28. A silent intervention

There is great power in silence. At times, it's harder to say or do nothing, than it is to say or do something. We're often too quick to react and to act, rather than just leave a silent pause, to see what emerges. There is such an imperative to respond and fill any void in a conversation, that much of the magic of 'what could be' can be lost.

What if someone pauses in conversation, and you just let it be? What would happen, if we chose not to engage in the social imperative to fill any gaps with more chatter? If we did not pack our conversations with so much content? What if people had time to muse, absorb, consider, and think – or to elaborate further on their thoughts, aloud. Would we end up with a better or worse result? Try it and see. Be brave with silence.

What if we just helped to make space for other people, rather than following our desire to fill the space, or fill the silence?

Could it be, that more often than not, the best kind of intervention is no intervention at all? A silent intervention.

Ingredients
Another person.
A pause.
The bravery to say nothing.

Method
1. Have coffee.
2. Have conversation.
3. When a pause occurs, don't feel that you have to fill the space.
4. Say nothing; allow it to be.
5. See what happens.

Reflections

Think back to a recent conversation. How often did you fill any gaps with words? How much silence was there?

In conversation, when a pause occurs, what if you simply waited? How will you feel? What might happen?

29. The ceremony

You might be familiar with the concept of Japanese tea ceremonies, but how about coffee ceremonies? There's more to coffee than grabbing a takeaway paper cup or a mug of instant, so try to add more ritual and ceremony to coffee experiences.

For example, coffee ceremonies are integral to Ethiopian social and cultural life. Offering an invitation to attend a coffee ceremony denotes respect or friendship and hospitality, and is to be received as such. Every part of the process is conducted in the same ritualised order, and every moment is savoured as special – almost mystical. You, too, can enjoy the ritual of your own coffees. Honour the person, and savour the moments – as well as the coffee – by being fully present and attentive.

The need for ceremony and ritual is almost a basic human instinct. With the falling away of organised religion in society, for many of us, there is a hole in our lives. The intention and emotional investment of adding ceremony and ritual into our daily interactions can fill that gap and dramatically improve our overall wellbeing.

Your own ceremony doesn't have to be an elaborate affair. You can even make it a ritual in your own head. It's more about the intention and the customary process than the rigid practice or outcome. You can ritualise the way you always greet your coffee guests – say, with a warm embrace. You can do something unobtrusive like taking a moment to relish the first look or taste of the coffee, or you can say something to yourself like a positive affirmation, mantra or prayer.

One simple ritual you could consider employing is to feel gratitude at the beginning or end of every conversation. There's a great deal of research that shows the positive benefits of having an attitude of gratitude. It's not just about thanking the person for their time – it's about truly feeling the emotion of gratitude – really being grateful for all of life's opportunities.

Build ritual and ceremony into your coffees, and develop your own ways of how you 'do coffee', whether that's by showing respect, enjoying mindfulness, giving thanks or whatever works for you. Like wearing your lucky pants.

No more instant coffee! Instead, enjoy a richer, more ritualised experience.

Ingredients
Your own ways of making ceremony or ritual.

Method
1. Have coffee.
2. Make it ceremonial.
3. Be mindful of the ritual.
4. Make it your custom.

Reflections

What sorts of daily or weekly rituals do you enjoy?

How can you make your coffee more 'ceremonial'? What routine or ritual will you maintain?

30. Bending time

Have you ever been 'in the moment' so strongly that time stood still? Or have you ever felt like a day passed in minutes? Do you remember how time passed when you were very young? And in comparison, how it passes now that you're older?

We assume that time is a linear concept, but our perception of time changes with age and situation. Mostly, this is an unconscious process, but in reality, we can deliberately bend time. Does that sound mind-bendingly strange? D'you think I'm round the bend to say this? Bear with me. Time will tell.

First of all, it's important to understand when these shifts in time perception happen in your own life, and then, you can use this knowledge to deliberately create them.

For me, time stands still when I'm in deep connection with another human being. An hour spent developing a close connection feels like days of growing intimacy to me, and yet, conversely, it seems to have flown by in seconds. You can be 'lost in time', yet be very present with the person. The more you create the environment in which connection can occur, the more time bends in your favour.

Could it be that the more you savour life, the more time seems to stand still? Does it happen more when you live 'in the moment', or when you're 'in the flow', doing things you love? When does it work in your favour? Can you replicate this feeling in other contexts?

In a world that is increasingly hurrying faster, being unconscious of how you perceive time means that a lot of it can slip through your fingers. Use your experience to be conscious of time – and see if you can shift the way you perceive it, to your benefit.

Ingredients
Time.
Noticing.

Method
1. Take your time.
2. Notice where it goes, and how it goes – fast or slowly.
3. Observe what you are doing when it goes slowly, stops, or works to your benefit.
4. Find ways to replicate how you achieve that, in other circumstances, when you need time to work in your favour.

Reflections

When does time 'drag' for you? What makes that happen?

____

____

____

When does time fly, for you? What makes that happen?

____

____

____

How can you use this knowledge to 'bend' time in your favour?

____

____

____

31. Eye contact

They say 'the eyes are the window into the soul'. Simple eye contact is a key way to foster a much deeper human connection with someone. The more you do this, the faster the process of connection. Your subconscious can process so much about another person, simply by looking them in the eyes. It is, however, a mutual exchange: to look someone in the eyes, they have to be looking you in the eyes. You both have to reveal yourselves. It's intimate, in a way. You might even feel exposed.

It isn't always easy, because your mind can resist this vulnerability and noisily protest. Feelings of judgement, fear, guilt, sadness or desire can all be apparent in the eyes. If you don't like being vulnerable, it's hard to maintain this contact – and the same applies to the person you're with. When someone cannot maintain eye contact with you, there's always a story behind it, so don't be offended and cut them some slack. The more compassionate you are to their story (even if they don't tell you it), the more they're able to maintain eye contact with you.

When we avert our gaze, or when someone else can't meet our eyes, it is because we/ they are self-conscious – afraid of revealing ourselves or of being judged. We might find it easier to look into the eyes of young children or animals, though – because we don't feel judged by them.

The Buddhist tradition (amongst others) uses deep, prolonged eye-gazing between people as a deep, healing practice. If you can, try to experience some form of eye-gazing healing. If you have never stared deeply and silently for 10 minutes into a stranger's eyes, you must try it. It might sound like a terrifying prospect, but once you have passed through the initial discomfort, there is something profoundly beautiful to be learned and experienced.

Develop this skill – and offer a safe space for others to have eye contact with you. It will lead you to a much richer and more connected life.

- How can you look people in the eyes more deeply and more often?
- If you are struggling to do this – or if you are with someone who is struggling – what are you learning?

Ingredients
Eyes – your own and someone else's.

Method
1. Look into someone's eyes:
    - while they are talking,
    - while you are talking,
    - while no-one is talking.
2. Observe your feelings, or what you perceive of their feelings.

Reflections

What colour were the eyes of the last five people you met?

When do you give lengthy eye contact to people? When don't you?

What do you feel when you look into someone's eyes?

The Coffee Network

32. Pay it forward

A tradition began in the working-class cafés of Naples: someone who'd experienced good luck would order a sospeso (suspended coffee). This means paying for two coffees but receiving and consuming only one. So, the price of a spare coffee has already been paid. Subsequently, a poor person, enquiring later if there was a sospeso available, would be served a pre-paid coffee, for free.

There is now a worldwide movement whereby coffee shops have adopted 'suspended coffees', not only to increase sales, but to promote kindness, sharing and caring. It's a way of paying forward – sharing your luck, and passing it on. And, just like this book, it's bigger than coffee, and can be applied to the rest of your life.

Everywhere I go, I try to adopt this principle. I carry 'Pay it Forward' cards with me and use any opportunities I can to help and encourage others. Whether I pay for a coffee or lunch for the person I'm meeting with, or if I drop off an extra coffee for a stranger in the cafe, I try to create opportunities to spread kindness.

Small acts of kindness and generosity can make someone's day, but they also give people a lasting impression of you as a human being. They say that first impressions count, but the small things you do matter just as much – if not more.

When I pay the bill, people often say, 'I'll get it next time'. I just tell them: 'Pay it forward', to encourage the kindness virus to spread wider to others, or in unusual ways. I often hand them a card to remind them to pass the good will on, even to a stranger. It's not just about buying coffee – it's any small act of kindness. And it's not just a transaction between two people for their mutual benefit – it's a chain reaction affecting many others. Kindness can spread a long way and transform people's lives.

Within every human interaction, you have the power to create acts of kindness – and to encourage other people, in turn, to pay it forward and pass good deeds onwards.

Make every interaction count. Blow people way with your kindness! Kindness is a far greater stimulant than any coffee you might drink. Try it – and see how high you get. It's truly energising – not least to think that you're making other people's lives better. Spread the joy.

Ingredients
One other person (coffee-mate or stranger).
One act of kindness.
Pay It Forward card (optional).

Method

1. Perform an act of kindness.
2. Ask the recipient to 'pay it forward' to someone else.
3. Enjoy the knowledge that you've spread the kindness.

'Pay it Forward' cards: https://payitforwardday.com/free-stuff/download-your-free-pay-it-forward-cards/

Reflections

List five random acts of kindness you could do for others.

Think of a time when you received a kindness. What was that like?

Think of a time when you did a kindness for someone. How did that feel?

33. The trust network

If one of your network has recommended that you should meet someone for coffee, there's usually some level of trust and connection with that person from the start. Six degrees of separation means that you are only 6 coffees away from any human being on the planet. In fact, research demonstrates that, owing to platforms like Facebook, the number of degrees of separation is falling to around 3.5. This means you're potentially only 3.5 conversations away from building trust with a key 'target' connection. In small communities, the degree of separation is more like 1.

When you've been introduced by someone else, you don't start the conversation as a total stranger. You've been endorsed by the individual who introduced you. That creates more trust and connection than if you were to 'cold call' or meet someone as a stranger.

If you want to meet with someone specific, with no introduction from a direct mutual connection, try to find a way to 'coffee your way' there, rather than contact them cold. Find someone who knows someone they know, and coffee them up. You know? It's much harder to reach out as a stranger – especially to busy people, or to experts with huge demands on their time. However, the more you foster deep relationships and profound connections with those you do meet, the more likely you are to be introduced, with trust, to other people.

Pushing people to meet you just doesn't work. Everyone hates a persistent cold-caller. If you want to meet someone specific, wait until they're ready; trusting and knowing that it's best for them to develop an equal desire to meet you and spend time with you. If their friends and colleagues mention your name with positivity or interest, meeting with you becomes a more attractive option. The path is laid out for you.

Above all, the objective of coffee is to just spend time with the person you're with. If you use coffee time solely to 'sell yourself' or persuade your coffee-mate to give you connections, you're missing the point of the exercise. That's more like business than pleasure. And this should be pure pleasure and fun.

Your focus in the moment is on the coffee you're currently having, and the person you're in conversation with at the present time. Getting an introduction to someone else through conversations is just a by-product of the trust and connection you cultivate with the first individual.

Hold the intention to meet the 'target' person you want to connect with ultimately, but do be mindful of how you set about approaching them.

Ingredients

One deep connection.
Network.
Six (or fewer) degrees of separation.
Trust.

Method

1. Connect deeply to create trust.
2. Build connections and networks.
3. Get introduced, or recommended, by mutual connections to interesting people.
4. Enjoy every coffee in the moment.

Reflections

Make a list of three to five people you really want to meet – and say why.

____

____

____

____

Note down ideas to join the dots between the '6 degrees of separation' and find the connections.

____

____

____

____

From your current connections, find the best 'route' to reach your targets.

34. The rule of 3

You can follow a little rule to bring you interesting results and interactions: the 'rule of 3'. It's very simple. If a certain person's name comes up 3 times in a series of recent conversations, you invite that person to go for coffee.

The invitation goes something like this: "Your name keeps coming up in conversation. It seems we have a lot of shared connections, and that must mean something. Would you be willing to go for coffee sometime?"

Frequently, this simple request gets a response. To some degree, most people are interested in patterns of coincidence (synchronicity) and hunches about meeting with no agenda. Most people are curious to discover what might occur from a meeting request with a little bit of magic in it.

You'll be surprised by the results of intuitive requests for coffee – they can be amazing! More value seems to come from these conversations than from typical ones. Follow your instincts to meet someone for no apparent reason whatsoever, and just see what occurs.

Start to observe this rule, learn to trust the signals – and follow the rule of 3. Try it and see what happens for you.

Ingredients
At least three coffee conversations.
One name (three mentions).

Method
1. Notice any individual's name that recurs across several conversations.
2. If one name is mentioned three times in different conversations, contact the named person and introduce yourself (using the phrasing above, or similar, observing the magic words – coincidence, synchronicity, fate, luck, seems like a sign to meet...)
3. Invite them for coffee.

Reflections

What pieces of luck, coincidences or 'chance meetings' have you had?

____

____

____

Look back on conversations over the last few months. Which names have come up more than twice? Are there any of these you haven't met – yet?

____

____

____

35. The connection virus

Much of what you're learning in this experiment is about creating a new way of being that's contagious!

In all of this, you're modelling a new type of behaviour to others that deepens and encourages human connection. This might be a subconscious rather than conscious action – but it still results in greater connection. Whether intentional on your part or not, this will inspire others to adopt the same behaviours.

We learn from those around us. You leave a legacy from the way you connect with others. Unconsciously, your influence will spread and others will change around you – and, as a result, they all impact on everyone they meet.

The deeper you connect with others, and the more consistently you demonstrate a connected way of being, the more you spread a 'virus of connection' in the world. No need to be afraid – you're not Typhoid Mary. It's a good virus, spreading goodness in a good way. It's all good.

When a number of you consistently adopt this practice of coffee connectivity,

you'll see this informal coffee style spreading in your own community and even wider. You'll see more and more informal conversations going on, taking things deeper; more friendships and partnerships developing as a result of the connection virus that's been released in your community.

This is so much more than just a different way of interacting with people. It's a form of leadership that fundamentally changes the world. Human connection is powerful, and like a virus, it will spread. Be a carrier!

Ingredients
Connection.

Method
1. Carry the connection.
2. Make it deep.
3. Spread it far and wide.

Reflections

What evidence is there of connectedness in your community?

How can you spread the connection virus even further?

36. Shifting realities

We all create our own reality, in life. As individuals, we're comfortable in our own beliefs, and we may choose to mix with people who think like us. Your coffees will challenge you, and take you out of your comfort zone. When differing beliefs, values or views emerge in conversation, it can cause friction between us and the person we're talking with. From divisions in our politics and religions, to diversity between nations and tribes – the world is subject to huge collective gaps in mutual understanding.

What's right? What's correct? What's true? What's real? We all hold on dearly to our own view of the world, as if it's the only version of reality that exists. We have this hugely strong attachment to 'what is' true/real to us, when 'what is' can never be the only version of reality in existence. Other people have other beliefs of what is 'true' or 'real' for them. And, as we experience new things, or appreciate 'new realities', our own beliefs and our current realities change, too. That's what I mean by shifting realities. Although you thought it was impossible, didn't you? Or that it involved the use of hallucinogenic drugs or too much coffee.

We need to find a way to transcend the realities we currently inhabit. Every belief system, every way of doing things, every lens on the world will be somehow disrupted in the years ahead.

Nothing is fixed; nothing is black and white – technology is transforming the world, and the impossible is becoming possible.

Chaos comes from us all sharing the same space whilst living in a mixture of realities, without understanding other people's beliefs, values or views (i.e. their reality). How can we ever understand one another and share our world, with so many diverse people with different realities they each hold to be true?

To create a shared reality, the super skills we all need to learn, are:

1. To hold someone's hand and help them to move gently on, from where they are.
2. To allow someone else to hold our hand to gently move us on, from where we are.

If, in coffee conversations, we spend time and energy developing these skills, we might find it a lot easier to get along, in life.

- How can you spend time in the other person's reality and let it influence your own?
- How can you gently influence another person's reality with your own wisdom?

Ingredients
Our reality.
Their reality.

Method

1. Be aware that your reality is not the only one.
2. Appreciate the other person's reality.
3. Join them in their reality, if you wish. Or invite them into yours.
4. Share the experience.

Reflections

What is your view of the world?

Think of someone with a different world view. How is their perception different?

What will it take for you to share one another's realities, for greater understanding and growth?

37. You are the people you spend time with

There's a great quote from Jim Rohn: "You are the average of the five people you spend the most time with." This is one of the most important things to consider, in transforming your life. If the people you spend time with don't mirror who you are, or who you want to become, you need to look at your networks and take the opportunity to change them. And yourself.

Reflecting on this and acting on it is a simple way to create change in your life. Consider all the areas of your life that you want to nourish – and in your coffees, make sure you reach out to people who embody your dearest beliefs, values, lifestyle and aspirations.

Spend time with people who are either models for you to follow, or fellow travellers on the magic carpet ride to who you want to be and where you want to go. Spend time with people who give you energy and who are aligned to your values, beliefs, hopes and aspirations. But don't be complacent, with 'like minds' or the same old tried and tested coffees. Try different flavours and styles. Also spend time with people who stretch and challenge you; who teach and improve you.

If you want to make a difference in the world – spend time with people making a difference. If you want to be healthy – spend time with people who are healthy. If you want to learn a new skill like public speaking – spend time with people who do this really well.

This is why coffee is a good thing. Getting to spend time with people of your own choosing is so liberating! It builds community and gives you confidence to take on whatever you want to do in the world.

The people you spend time with can be great assets to your life. Be intentional in your choice of friends, colleagues and coffee-mates, and use the premise that 'you are who you connect with' to take you places.

Ingredients

People of like minds.
People you aspire to be like.
Lots of coffees.

Method

1. Look at who you mix with – are they who you want to be?
2. Mix with people you like/want to be like/who have skills, experience, lives and qualities you aspire to have.
3. Learn from them, or be like them – as well as remaining your unique self.

Reflections

Who are the people you spend time with? Do they nourish you, teach you, or challenge you?

____

____

____

____

Who do you want to be? What skills, values, qualities and experiences do you aspire to have?

____

____

____

____

Who are your role models – the people you need to spend more time with?

____

____

____

____

____

38. Dunbar's number

Dunbar's number is the maximum number of stable social relationships one can cognitively maintain. That is – who's in your head, and who's actively involved in your life? The average often quoted is 150 relationships, although it does vary, depending on the individual and their collective capacity. Dunbar's number commonly appears in analyses of communities that lose cohesion and break up into smaller groups. If the group's too big, it can't function.

This phenomenon stems from our hunter-gatherer days, but it's still very much relevant in our everyday life. Many people are using this number to limit the size of organisations and groups, to maximise effectiveness. It's one of the main reasons why outsourcing works so well.

In building your coffee network and maintaining it, think about how to utilise this number. Here, we're starting with 50 – but who knows how many other coffees you'll have and connections you'll make along the way? How much caffeine can you take? Which connections will you maintain, and which people will you collaborate with, in work or play, or in your life mission? Whatever you wish to achieve in life, you need a tribe of deep relationships to achieve it.

People talk about scalability, but scaling relationships isn't very human.. You can successfully scale businesses, but there's a point at which the larger scale disconnects you from the people you serve, and you end up simply building a big machine. And machines just don't make people as happy as closer human relationships do. It's just not the way our brains are built.

So the first question for you to consider is:
- How can you develop a manageable number of deep human relationships, whilst impacting many more lives in the process?

And the second question is:
- What part can going for coffee play in cultivating and developing your tribe?

Re the questions, how can you manage your life and maximise relationships, to maximum effect?

Ingredients
Your relationships.
Awareness.

Method
1. Look at your relationship network/s.
2. Recognise your limits, in terms of effective relationships.
3. Identify better ways to manage and progress these.
4. Review and revise.

Reflections

List the people with whom you have an effective relationship. And those with whom you need to build closer relationships.

____

____

____

____

____

How can you manage or grow your relationships, to maximise their impact on the world?

---

39. Emergence

Over the past few years, new ways of thinking and being have emerged, and fundamental shifts have happened – all as a result of conversations with people. Could anyone have predicted this? Absolutely not.

When we don't understand how things could possibly happen, we struggle to predict them – and yet we all know that 'unpredictable' things happen in our lives. We might as well predict unpredictability! However, human beings struggle with that ambiguity.

This 'emergence' of new thinking and being is a really positive thing. We can benefit greatly from knowing that new, currently unimaginable wonders will eventually emerge. It gives us hope and helps us to step forward into the unknown.

And in many ways, that's what this adventure is all about. You might start with some desired outcome at the beginning (even though I told you not to have an outcome in mind – naughty!), but something completely different – something that you could never have conceived – might emerge.

That's why you are encouraged to have no expectations of particular outcomes for coffees, but leave yourself open yourself to any possibilities.

- Are you open to starting something, just to see what emerges?
- Are you open to unexpected outcomes on your journey?
- Can you handle the unpredictable?

Set sail, have plenty of coffees, and see what emerges.

Ingredients

Openness.

Method

1. Start something.
2. Predict the unpredictable.
3. Allow things to emerge.
4. See what happens.

Reflections

Since your youth – what unimaginable innovations or unpredictable things have emerged or occurred?

____

____

____

____

If you imagine being able to 'predict the unpredictable' – how will that change you, or your life?

____

____

____

____

The Coffee Break

40. Learn how to receive

In meeting people over coffee, one of the challenges some people face is learning to receive the generosity of others. From accepting kind words and compliments, to letting others pay the bill, to allowing people to do things for you – it might take some time for you to receive these gladly. Or your coffee-mate might feel this resistance. You might feel an urge to argue, fight, deny, disbelieve and contradict them – all actions of conflict. This is the opposite to what you want to achieve, which is connection.

An inability to accept the generosity of others is a barrier to human connection. In some cases, the person offering the kindness can feel rejected or unvalued if you don't accept their offer.

If it doesn't come naturally to you, learning to receive is a vital skill that needs to be learnt. The biggest reframe is to understand that accepting someone's generosity with good grace is a real gift to them, because it makes them feel good. If you love being in your generosity zone, this helps you to feel generous when people are being generous to you.

Of course, this doesn't mean that you have to accept something that you genuinely don't want. Whether that's a word of harsh criticism, a job, a proposal of marriage, a life-size stuffed elephant, or another cup of coffee. You can always say no.

Just be mindful that learning to receive well serves you well. Be generous enough to receive, graciously.

Ingredients
Someone giving you something.
The grace to receive.

Method
1.   Allow yourself to receive.

Reflections

Think of a time when someone has given you a kindness, or been generous. How did you feel? How did you react? What happened?

____

____

____

____

How will you receive in future, with more grace?

____

____

____

____

41. Keep your promises

The objective of your Coffee Adventure is to deepen your connection with people. Much of this comes from trust. We all have conversations with people, and we often make them offers of help, information, or action. The important thing is to record the promises you make at the time – and deliver on them at the earliest opportunity. No ifs; no buts.

Every time you fail in a promise, you leak trust and devalue the connection you've made; so it's really important for you to develop a bulletproof personal system to use in your Coffee Adventure.

It takes a lot of mental bandwidth to keep everything in your mind: we can easily forget. Developing a fail-safe system that doesn't rely on your mind and your memory is vital.

Some people use notebooks or a smartphone task list. It doesn't matter what method you use, as long you capture your promises 100% of the time, and deliver 100% of the time. If you forget a promise even once, this means that your personal system is fallible and needs to be redesigned, to work for you.

Know what you can deliver on 100%, and be careful to only make promises you can keep. You needn't be rigid in how you help people, but do make sure you're rigid in delivering on what you offer. If you have a heavy coffee-load, you needn't promise more than an email with a link to useful information or an introduction to another coffee-mate. If you do over-promise and find yourself unable to do something, send an email apologising and explain why you can't fulfil the promise.

Be careful not to hold any grudge or malice if others don't deliver on their promises, either. Other people don't necessarily have strong personal systems, so don't blame them. It might be best to capture the promises they make to you, and remind them in an e-mail, to clarify. Most failures to deliver are a failure of system, rather than a failure of the individual – and this belief helps you to be more compassionate.

Recognise, too, that no outcome is needed from a coffee. A conversation without any promise or commitment is just fine. Simply ensure that if you do make an offer, you always deliver.

The simple truth is – if you know you can't deliver, don't make the promise. Being realistic about your workload or commitments, or choosing to spend time with your family and friends, is just fine. People will trust you more if you're honest about your reality. What breaks trust is saying one thing and doing another – or over-promising and under-delivering. Far better to surprise someone with more than they expect, if you can.

The final note is on clarity of language. At the end of the conversation, be clear about what you will do for someone. 'I will do x. I will do y.' Whatever you are offering, make it obvious. Don't be grey or ambiguous in your language – be crystal clear, to prevent misperception or misunderstanding.

Trust is currency. Increase yours by keeping your promises. It's a great investment.

Ingredients

Bulletproof system for turning words into action.
A sprinkle of goodwill, seasoned with realism.
Promise (if capable).
Action (if promised).
Clear language.

Method

1. Be realistic, and only make promises you can fulfill.
2. Make it clear what you're offering.
3. Record a promise.
4. Turn it into action.
5. Forgive those who don't deliver.
6. Enjoy greater trust and connectedness.

Reflections

Think about the last few weeks. Have you said you would do something for somebody? Did you deliver?

____

____

____

____

____

What promises have you made? How easy were they to keep?

____

____

____

____

____

How will you ensure that you manage, and deliver, tasks or promises?

---

42. Sharing with integrity

Openness and connectedness bring greater depth and quality to the information you learn about people. But having coffee also requires integrity and confidence, for inviting sharing and receiving information from others in a space of vulnerability.

In many communities, gossip can be traded as a commodity, with people gaining status from how much they know about people and whatever is going on with them.

This project is not about you achieving status. It is about you creating more trust and connectedness within a community you build for yourself. The key to becoming a more trusted and valued community member is how you deal with the responsibility of holding knowledge about people.

Unless you're told to keep something confidential, maybe you don't think it should be kept private. Sharing information about people can be very helpful, but it can create issues, too. You should be purposeful, at all times, with what you share and why you share it.

- Does this information support the life of the person you are talking about?
- Would your sharing, and the way you have shared it, be acceptable to the individual concerned?
- Would you say it to the person's face?
- Is this information-sharing building the community, or driving it apart?

Whether it's a confession about smelly feet or an unhappy marriage – whether it's sensitive business ideas or a funny anecdote – use your judgement about which information can be shared. When in doubt, keep quiet. Loose lips cost coffees. It should go without saying that things told to you explicitly in confidence should not be shared. Spill the beans, and you've completely wasted the coffee. And perhaps irreparably damaged relationships. Trust matters, above all.

The aim of connected coffeeing is to weave the fabric of society together, rather than tear it apart. When you're considering whether or not to share information about other human beings, it's really important to come from a place of deep integrity and respect for the person who shared that information with you, in trust. Know when to keep information to yourself.

Seek always to improve the lives of others through the information you do share.

Ingredients
Information.
Integrity.
Openness.
Community focus.

Method
1. First, take a generous helping of integrity.
2. Blend together conversation with judicious information, as appropriate.
3. Ensure that all ingredients are combined well with integrity, for a successful result.

Reflections

Has anyone betrayed your trust or shared a confidence? How did it feel? How could you have prevented it?

How do you know if information is to be shared – or not?

____

____

____

____

How will you ensure that you share with integrity?

____

____

____

____

43. Technology and distractions

Oh, those embarrassing ringtones! Even an unexpected vibration in your trouser pocket can throw you for six. But once you know there's a message, it's hard not to take your phone out to see what it's about. Trying to have a conversation without getting distracted by your technology can be difficult. We have access to news, messages, emails, posts and phone-calls at all times.

Of course, technology can help you with coffee. Not just through a state-of-the art coffee-machine – you can also have virtual   coffees via Facetime, Skype and Zoom, and maintain connections through email, phone and social media. Distraction and interruption by technology during your coffees are the problems.

When the objective of a coffee is to go deeper, to foster a lasting connection, anything that pulls you out of that conversation is a barrier to the primary objective. It takes time to go deep, and every small distraction brings you back to the surface. If they occur regularly, they'll prevent you from reaching any depth at all. Checking your texts and emails, or answering your phone, all send a very strong message to the other person that 'You're not as important as whatever else is going on in my life'.

What you do about this depends on your relationship with your technology. If you're someone who simply can't leave it alone, then design systems and use approaches that help you to ignore it. Most smartphones have settings to minimise disturbances when you don't want them. Believe it or not, you can even switch phones off! OMG!

You can be more creative in tackling these challenges. When you're out with friends for a meal or drinks, you could put all your phones in the middle of the table. The first person to grab their phone has to pay the bill! How's that for a disincentive?

Be conscious of the effects of technology on your life. Are you using it as a tool to improve your life? To increase connection with those around you? Or is the technology actually taking you away from what's possible?

Get your relationship with technology right, and you can really go places. Get it wrong and you can stay plugged into the matrix – missing the joy of what is in the moment.

Ingredients
Technology (phone, tablet, laptop).

Method
Remove or deactivate all ingredients.

Reflections

What distracts you from connecting with people face-to-face? How much time do you spend 'distracted' from real-life connection?

How can you minimise the distractions? What do you need to do to avoid interruptions or technology?

The Coffee Machine

44. The 80/20 rule

One of the greatest rules for success is the 80/20 rule, also known as the Pareto Principle. This states that 20% of your effort is likely to deliver 80% of your results. It's a universal rule that can be applied to most areas of life and business.

Knowing where to concentrate your effort for maximum benefit is the key to greater effectiveness in life.

Building relationships over coffee is important because most of the results you achieve come from the relationships you nurture and develop, rather than from the work you do. So, do a quick check. You might be spending only a fraction of your time developing what really matters, and most of your time doing things that deliver a fraction of the results.

Shift to spending most of your time working on and developing relationships, and your results can accelerate. Use the 80/20 rule to remodel your time and effort to deliver higher value aspects of life.

If you apply the 80/20 rule to all aspects of your life, you will experience great transformation.

Pay it forward. Give other people an insight into the 80/20 rule, and you'll help them to achieve what they want in life, too. Ask yourself:

- Where do the greatest results in my life actually come from?
- How much of my time and effort actually goes towards delivering those results?

Ingredients
20% effort; or,
20% time.

Method
1. Check how much time you spend enjoying company or connecting with people.
2. Check how much time you spend on doing things that get you results.
3. Analyse, and adjust.

Reflections

Where does your happiness come from?

How much time are you actually spending there?

How can you spend more time on what really matters?

45. The overlapping Coffee

Book your coffees back to back. That way, you create situations in which coffees can overlap. When you're finishing one conversation and you see the next person arrives, don't let them shuffle off into a corner, embarrassed, thinking they've got the time wrong and sullenly waiting for you to finish. Greet them and welcome them over. And don't let your first coffee-mate hurry off like a caffeine-charged sprinter. Hold onto them, although not literally, unless they are actually sprinting… Create the space for a 10 – 15 minute conversation when two people from separate coffees get to meet each other and make a connection.

Introduce them by celebrating each one's strengths and interests and explaining why they might find each other interesting. Then allow a few minutes for a shared conversation, if it feels right. If there seems to be a strong connection, connect them both by e-mail and encourage them to meet each other for coffee.

Not only is it really beneficial for us to make deep personal connections: it's also great to create new ones for others. Since the focus of these coffees is on deeper conversation, it's a great gift to connect two other people from that place, too. It creates strong initial connections for people, right from the beginning.

The simple act of letting coffees overlap can create some amazing connections, friendships and collaborations.

A super incredible way to create something from nothing!

Ingredients
Two coffees.
No time between them.
Enthusiasm.
Facts about each person's interests, strengths and points of commonality.

Method
1. Ensure that one coffee ends just as your next one arrives.
2. Introduce each with enthusiasm, and stir for a few minutes.
3. Let conversation flow for a few minutes, if it does.
4. If appropriate, hook them up.
5. Let whatever will be, be.

Reflections

**Think of 3 significant persons. How were you first introduced?
How was the connection developed?**

____

____

____

**Which of your coffee-mates really should meet one another?
How will you arrange this?**

____

____

____

46. The open calendar

Be bold, and run an experiment for a year. Open-source your calendar to the world and allow anyone to book a coffee appointment with you, wherever you are. You can have also virtual coffees by Skype, Facetime and Zoom. Offer coffees to the world. Are you frightened, or excited? Have a coffee, anyway.

You can completely give up strategizing about who you're going to see, and why. Share your open calendar on social media, or on your blog, and e-mail it to everyone you know, making yourself available for coffee to anyone who wants it.

You'll be surprised by the increased richness it brings to your life. Everyone you meet is ready for a conversation and has something interesting to say. The synchronicities that can occur through adopting this approach are quite profound. Unexpected conversations you wouldn't have had otherwise will help you to see the world in different ways. It will be singularly one of the most interesting learning experiences of your life. It was, for me!

The process teaches you that the more you restrict the way you travel through life, the more you restrict the magic that life can bring you.

The extra bonus of allowing people to book into your calendar directly is a reduction in administrative burden. Many platforms and booking systems allow you to do this.

No phone-calls or emails back and forth, or PAs checking diary availability and confirming agendas. Just coffee – direct.

When you're always meeting in busy coffee shops, you're always safe. Expect very few cancellations and no-shows. Overwhelmingly, people really value and make good use of your time – and you will gain a great deal from these coffees. You can make this a permanent part of how you do things. Sure, you can still be intentional about who you see and why, but be open to see anyone else, when you have the time and space to do so.

Everyone should consider doing this in some way – either through offering a 'Free Friday morning', an 'open week' or a completely open calendar.

Open up to the world unconditionally, and allow yourself access to experiences and conversations you otherwise would not have. Open up to opportunity!

Ingredients
One open public calendar or diary.
Several outlets to promote it: social media, email.
Boundless recipients.
Coffee bar, Zoom link or public meeting space.
Open mind.

Method
1. Make sure your diary or calendar is visible and accessible to the public.
2. Tell people via social media, emails, blogs and other means that you are open to coffee meetings and to book via your public calendar (with link).
3. Watch for coffees to appear on your calendar.
4. Attend the coffees.
5. Let the magic happen.

Reflections

How can you make yourself available for Open coffees?

____

____

____

____

____

What needs to happen, to meet new people you don't know?

____

____

____

____

47. Missing appointments

If you attend several coffees a week, you need a good system to maintain them. It takes quite an investment of time and energy to co-ordinate 50 coffees, and unless you're organised, things can go wrong, with so many meeting invitations flying around.

Establish a very good personal system for organising things. Any time you experience a calendar error, work out why and develop ways to make sure it doesn't happen again. Work on reducing your failure rates.

Treat every appointment as a promise – and commit to it. Try your best to ensure you're there on time. Aim to never cancel or move an appointment.

The failure rate of other people you meet can be higher. Maybe 1 in 10 coffees might cancel within 48 hours, or be no-shows. There's a huge variance in the organisational systems that people operate, so don't expect everyone to be as efficient as you. The busier people are, or the more they rely on their mind and memory to run their life, the greater the likelihood of error or issues.

If people don't show up, are late, or if they keep cancelling, don't let it trigger you. Recognise that failures to show have many reasons: poor personal systems, different priorities, genuine human issues, or busyness. Always assume that the reason is innocent, not personal. You're usually right to give people the benefit of the doubt. It's a system failure, not a personal failure. The majority of people in the world are just not productivity ninjas like you!

Always take something to do while you're waiting, so no time is ever wasted. Every missed or cancelled appointment becomes an opening of opportunity you can cherish and utilise. Your time will always be used effectively. Whether you're reading, working, crocheting or learning to play the keyboard, there's always something you can do. Maybe take headphones if you ARE learning to play the keyboard, so you can do it without disturbing people. Not everyone in a coffee shop appreciates music. Especially not from learners.

Be proactive in organising coffee. Assume that e-mails sometimes get missed, so if you don't get a response, keep going until you meet the person. You can allow, say, 2 failures, errors or issues with individuals before you become less proactive. Some people are just not ready or able to meet, and that's just fine.

The more reliable you are, the better you can build trust and connect with people. The more your systems work without relying on storing details and dates in your mind, the more freedom you'll have to enjoy life. Having lots of meetings and lots of conversations takes a lot of mental bandwidth. Get good at operating in this coffee world without it becoming a hardship.

If people are late or 'stand you up', take the opportunity to just let it go and be compassionate. Use this 50-coffee opportunity to develop a resilient organisational system that works for you all the time, every time. It will change your life.

Ingredients
A good system.
Several coffees.
Something to do while waiting – a book, some work, your laptop, a potter's wheel.
Compassion.

Method

1. Arrange coffees, using your system.
2. Keep your promise to meet on time.
3. Keep busy while you wait – 'spare' time is a bonus!
4. Forgive others' 'failures' to meet – it's not about you; it's human error or circumstances beyond their control.
5. Review and refine your system for better organisation, better connections, and a better life!

Reflections

What's your bullet-proof system for: 1) inviting; 2) scheduling/recording; 3) reminding; 4) meeting; and 5) maximising coffee?

1) inviting

2) scheduling/recording

3) reminding

4) meeting

5) maximising

48. The gentle nudge

What do you do, when you ask someone for coffee and you don't hear back from them? Shout at them? Cry? Knock at their door and demand to know why? When nothing happens after you've sent a message to invite someone for coffee, follow up with a gentle reminder that goes something like this:

'Hey, X, I didn't hear from you about this. Let me know if you are interested in catching up for coffee. It would be great to spend time with you. Y.'

Rather than believing that your request has been rejected, assume that people are busy and are just not great at e-mailing. 90% of the time, that assumption is right.

A gentle nudge or reminder can get a lot of people to respond to you, so it's always worth trying it, to see what response you get.

Recognise that people are busy, and it isn't always the right time. Don't sweat over that stuff. Focus on building your network and community where it's easier, rather than hard.

Proactively ask people to meet up for coffee, but don't dwell on it if they're not ready or willing to do so. Certainly don't take it to heart. There are over 7 billion people out there, and so many incredible conversations you've yet to have!

Ingredients
A reminder.
Resilience.

Method
1. If you don't hear back from someone, remind them.
2. Meet, or move on.

Reflections

How will you gently nudge people? How many times?

If they don't respond, what will you do next?

49. Kindness to those who serve

When we're deeply immersed in conversation, we often forget about the great work that goes into creating the environment around us, where the conversation is taking place. If you're in a coffee bar or cafe, the servers, cashiers, counter staff and waiters can become a blur in the background, if you're not careful.

Being fully connected to our companion but disconnected from those serving us means we miss the opportunity to spread the gift of human connection even further.

It's a beautiful sight to watch a person being kind to someone else. Every time I see it, I fall in love with the person showing kindness. Understand that sharing kindness beyond your coffee-mate and demonstrating it to others doesn't take away from the experience. It actually adds to it.

Many people who work in service industries have thankless tasks to do. Be the one

who thanks them. Be the one who helps them to 'Have a good day!' They are not only doing their job; they're helping you in your own quest by setting the scene, serving you coffee and maintaining the ambience.

What does it take, to show appreciation to those who serve? That extra word or two? That deeper, more sincere 'thank you'? That moment of eye contact? Spend a moment appreciating what they do, connecting with them, and you will give and receive a greater deal in return.

Take the time to be kind to those who serve. It will serve you well.

Ingredients
Server/s.
Kindness.
A moment to connect.

Method
1. Take a moment.
2. Show kindness, and connect with your server.

Reflections

How often do you appreciate 'those who serve'? How do you show it?

____

____

____

How can you show more appreciation?

____

____

____

50. Do you have a recipe of your own?

This challenge is designed to create a worldwide community of people all sharing a 50 Coffee Adventure. The recipes in this adventure are based on extensive research and opportunities for improving the art of going for coffee.

This is by no means an exhaustive list – it's your starting point. It is hoped that the list of recipes will get bigger and better over time – with your experimentation, assistance and contribution.

Ingredients
A coffee.
An idea to make it work.

Method
1. Come up with a new recipe/idea for having coffee OR experiment while you are having coffee.
2. Try it out.
3. If it works, enjoy it.
4. If it doesn't work, adapt it for greater success, or start again at 1.

Reflections

What's been the best conversation you've had? Analyse the elements that made it good.

____

____

____

____

____

What tips would you give someone for successful coffee conversations, to build connections?

Write your own recipe

Title:

Introduction/ rationale:

Ingredients:

Method:

Reflective questions:

THE 50 COFFEE ADVENTURE NUMBER (1)

Date and time: ___________________ **Location:** ___________________

Person: ___________________

What did I learn from the experience of having this coffee? ___________________

____

How has it changed the way I see the world? ___________________

____

How will it change the way I move forward? ___________________

____

What can I learn from this, to impact my mission? ___________________

____

Was there anything that triggered discomfort in this conversation? And why? ___________________

____

What commitments did I make, that I need to act on? ___________________

____

How could I improve the way I have coffee? ___________________

____

Are there any other people I need to have coffee with, as a result of this conversation?

____

____

____

THE 50 COFFEE ADVENTURE NUMBER (2)

Date and time: ________________________ **Location:** ________________________

Person: ____

What did I learn from the experience of having this coffee?

____

How has it changed the way I see the world?

____

How will it change the way I move forward?

____

What can I learn from this, to impact my mission?

____

Was there anything that triggered discomfort in this conversation? And why?

____

What commitments did I make, that I need to act on?

____

How could I improve the way I have coffee?

____

Are there any other people I need to have coffee with, as a result of this conversation?

____

____

____

THE 50 COFFEE ADVENTURE NUMBER ③

Date and time: ___________________________ **Location:** ___________________

Person: ____

What did I learn from the experience of having this coffee? ________________

____

How has it changed the way I see the world? _____________________________

____

How will it change the way I move forward? _______________________________

____

What can I learn from this, to impact my mission? _________________________

____

Was there anything that triggered discomfort in this conversation? And why? ___

____

What commitments did I make, that I need to act on? ______________________

____

How could I improve the way I have coffee? _______________________________

____

Are there any other people I need to have coffee with, as a result of this conversation?

____

____

____

THE 50 COFFEE ADVENTURE NUMBER  4

Date and time: _______________________ **Location:** ___________________

Person: ____

What did I learn from the experience of having this coffee? ________________

____

How has it changed the way I see the world? ____________________________

____

How will it change the way I move forward? _____________________________

____

What can I learn from this, to impact my mission? _______________________

____

Was there anything that triggered discomfort in this conversation? And why?

____

What commitments did I make, that I need to act on? _____________________

____

How could I improve the way I have coffee? _____________________________

____

Are there any other people I need to have coffee with, as a result of this conversation?

____

____

____

THE 50 COFFEE ADVENTURE NUMBER (5)

Date and time: **Location:**

Person:

What did I learn from the experience of having this coffee?

How has it changed the way I see the world?

How will it change the way I move forward?

What can I learn from this, to impact my mission?

Was there anything that triggered discomfort in this conversation? And why?

What commitments did I make, that I need to act on?

How could I improve the way I have coffee?

Are there any other people I need to have coffee with, as a result of this conversation?

THE 50 COFFEE ADVENTURE NUMBER (6)

Date and time: ________________________ **Location:** ________________________

Person: ____

What did I learn from the experience of having this coffee? ________________________

____

How has it changed the way I see the world? ____

____

How will it change the way I move forward? ____

____

What can I learn from this, to impact my mission? ____________________________________

____

Was there anything that triggered discomfort in this conversation? And why? ____________

____

What commitments did I make, that I need to act on? __________________________________

____

How could I improve the way I have coffee? ____

____

Are there any other people I need to have coffee with, as a result of this conversation?

____

____

____

THE 50 COFFEE ADVENTURE NUMBER 7

Date and time: _______________________ **Location:** _______________________

Person: _______________________

What did I learn from the experience of having this coffee?

____

How has it changed the way I see the world?

____

How will it change the way I move forward?

____

What can I learn from this, to impact my mission?

____

Was there anything that triggered discomfort in this conversation? And why?

____

What commitments did I make, that I need to act on?

____

How could I improve the way I have coffee?

____

Are there any other people I need to have coffee with, as a result of this conversation?

____

____

____

THE 50 COFFEE ADVENTURE NUMBER  8

Date and time: _______________________ **Location:** _______________________

Person: ____

What did I learn from the experience of having this coffee?
____

How has it changed the way I see the world?
____

How will it change the way I move forward?
____

What can I learn from this, to impact my mission?
____

Was there anything that triggered discomfort in this conversation? And why?
____

What commitments did I make, that I need to act on?
____

How could I improve the way I have coffee?
____

Are there any other people I need to have coffee with, as a result of this conversation?
____
____

THE 50 COFFEE ADVENTURE NUMBER (9)

Date and time: _______________________   **Location:** _______________________

Person: _______________________

What did I learn from the experience of having this coffee?
____

How has it changed the way I see the world?
____

How will it change the way I move forward?
____

What can I learn from this, to impact my mission?
____

Was there anything that triggered discomfort in this conversation? And why?
____

What commitments did I make, that I need to act on?
____

How could I improve the way I have coffee?
____

Are there any other people I need to have coffee with, as a result of this conversation?
____
____
____

THE 50 COFFEE ADVENTURE NUMBER  10

Date and time: ___________________________ **Location:** ___________________

Person: ____

What did I learn from the experience of having this coffee? ___________________

____

How has it changed the way I see the world? ________________________________

____

How will it change the way I move forward? ________________________________

____

What can I learn from this, to impact my mission? ___________________________

____

Was there anything that triggered discomfort in this conversation? And why? _____

____

What commitments did I make, that I need to act on? ________________________

____

How could I improve the way I have coffee? ________________________________

____

Are there any other people I need to have coffee with, as a result of this conversation?

____

____

____

THE 50 COFFEE ADVENTURE NUMBER (11)

Date and time: **Location:**

Person:

What did I learn from the experience of having this coffee?

How has it changed the way I see the world?

How will it change the way I move forward?

What can I learn from this, to impact my mission?

Was there anything that triggered discomfort in this conversation? And why?

What commitments did I make, that I need to act on?

How could I improve the way I have coffee?

Are there any other people I need to have coffee with, as a result of this conversation?

THE 50 COFFEE ADVENTURE NUMBER (12)

Date and time: ________________________ **Location:** ________________________

Person: ____

What did I learn from the experience of having this coffee? ________________
____

How has it changed the way I see the world? ________________________________
____

How will it change the way I move forward? _________________________________
____

What can I learn from this, to impact my mission? __________________________
____

Was there anything that triggered discomfort in this conversation? And why? __
____

What commitments did I make, that I need to act on? ________________________
____

How could I improve the way I have coffee? _________________________________
____

Are there any other people I need to have coffee with, as a result of this conversation?
____
____
____

THE 50 COFFEE ADVENTURE NUMBER (13)

Date and time: **Location:**

Person:

What did I learn from the experience of having this coffee?

How has it changed the way I see the world?

How will it change the way I move forward?

What can I learn from this, to impact my mission?

Was there anything that triggered discomfort in this conversation? And why?

What commitments did I make, that I need to act on?

How could I improve the way I have coffee?

Are there any other people I need to have coffee with, as a result of this conversation?

THE 50 COFFEE ADVENTURE NUMBER  **14**

Date and time: ___________________________ **Location:** _______________

Person: ____

What did I learn from the experience of having this coffee?

____

How has it changed the way I see the world?

____

How will it change the way I move forward?

____

What can I learn from this, to impact my mission?

____

Was there anything that triggered discomfort in this conversation? And why?

____

What commitments did I make, that I need to act on?

____

How could I improve the way I have coffee?

____

Are there any other people I need to have coffee with, as a result of this conversation?

____

____

____

THE 50 COFFEE ADVENTURE NUMBER  15

Date and time: **Location:**

Person:

What did I learn from the experience of having this coffee?

How has it changed the way I see the world?

How will it change the way I move forward?

What can I learn from this, to impact my mission?

Was there anything that triggered discomfort in this conversation? And why?

What commitments did I make, that I need to act on?

How could I improve the way I have coffee?

Are there any other people I need to have coffee with, as a result of this conversation?

THE 50 COFFEE ADVENTURE NUMBER 

Date and time: ___________________________ **Location:** ___________________

Person: ____

What did I learn from the experience of having this coffee? ________________

____

How has it changed the way I see the world? _______________________________

____

How will it change the way I move forward? _______________________________

____

What can I learn from this, to impact my mission? __________________________

____

Was there anything that triggered discomfort in this conversation? And why? __

____

What commitments did I make, that I need to act on? _______________________

____

How could I improve the way I have coffee? ________________________________

____

Are there any other people I need to have coffee with, as a result of this conversation?

____

____

THE 50 COFFEE ADVENTURE NUMBER (17)

Date and time: ________________________ **Location:** ________________________

Person: ____

What did I learn from the experience of having this coffee? ____________________

____

How has it changed the way I see the world? __________________________________

____

How will it change the way I move forward? __________________________________

____

What can I learn from this, to impact my mission? ____________________________

____

Was there anything that triggered discomfort in this conversation? And why? ______

____

What commitments did I make, that I need to act on? __________________________

____

How could I improve the way I have coffee? __________________________________

____

Are there any other people I need to have coffee with, as a result of this conversation?

____

____

____

THE 50 COFFEE ADVENTURE NUMBER (18)

Date and time: ________________ **Location:** ________________

Person: ________________

What did I learn from the experience of having this coffee? ________________

____

How has it changed the way I see the world? ________________

____

How will it change the way I move forward? ________________

____

What can I learn from this, to impact my mission? ________________

____

Was there anything that triggered discomfort in this conversation? And why? ________

____

What commitments did I make, that I need to act on? ________________

____

How could I improve the way I have coffee? ________________

____

Are there any other people I need to have coffee with, as a result of this conversation?

____

____

THE 50 COFFEE ADVENTURE NUMBER (19)

Date and time: ___________________________ **Location:** ___________________

Person: ____

What did I learn from the experience of having this coffee? _______________

____

How has it changed the way I see the world? ____________________________

____

How will it change the way I move forward? _____________________________

____

What can I learn from this, to impact my mission? _______________________

____

Was there anything that triggered discomfort in this conversation? And why? ___

____

What commitments did I make, that I need to act on? _____________________

____

How could I improve the way I have coffee? _____________________________

____

Are there any other people I need to have coffee with, as a result of this conversation?

____

____

____

THE 50 COFFEE ADVENTURE NUMBER (20)

Date and time: _______________________ **Location:** _______________________

Person: ____

What did I learn from the experience of having this coffee?

____

How has it changed the way I see the world?

____

How will it change the way I move forward?

____

What can I learn from this, to impact my mission?

____

Was there anything that triggered discomfort in this conversation? And why?

____

What commitments did I make, that I need to act on?

____

How could I improve the way I have coffee?

____

Are there any other people I need to have coffee with, as a result of this conversation?

____

____

____

THE 50 COFFEE ADVENTURE NUMBER (21)

Date and time: **Location:**

Person:

What did I learn from the experience of having this coffee?

How has it changed the way I see the world?

How will it change the way I move forward?

What can I learn from this, to impact my mission?

Was there anything that triggered discomfort in this conversation? And why?

What commitments did I make, that I need to act on?

How could I improve the way I have coffee?

Are there any other people I need to have coffee with, as a result of this conversation?

THE 50 COFFEE ADVENTURE NUMBER (22)

Date and time: ___________________ **Location:** ___________________

Person: ___________________

What did I learn from the experience of having this coffee? ___________________

____

How has it changed the way I see the world? ___________________

____

How will it change the way I move forward? ___________________

____

What can I learn from this, to impact my mission? ___________________

____

Was there anything that triggered discomfort in this conversation? And why? ___________________

____

What commitments did I make, that I need to act on? ___________________

____

How could I improve the way I have coffee? ___________________

____

Are there any other people I need to have coffee with, as a result of this conversation? ___________________

____

____

____

THE 50 COFFEE ADVENTURE NUMBER  23

Date and time: **Location:**

Person:

What did I learn from the experience of having this coffee?

How has it changed the way I see the world?

How will it change the way I move forward?

What can I learn from this, to impact my mission?

Was there anything that triggered discomfort in this conversation? And why?

What commitments did I make, that I need to act on?

How could I improve the way I have coffee?

Are there any other people I need to have coffee with, as a result of this conversation?

THE 50 COFFEE ADVENTURE NUMBER 

24

Date and time: ________________________ **Location:** ________________________

Person: ____

What did I learn from the experience of having this coffee? ________________

____

How has it changed the way I see the world? ______________________________

____

How will it change the way I move forward? _______________________________

____

What can I learn from this, to impact my mission? _________________________

____

Was there anything that triggered discomfort in this conversation? And why? ___

____

What commitments did I make, that I need to act on? _______________________

____

How could I improve the way I have coffee? _______________________________

____

Are there any other people I need to have coffee with, as a result of this conversation?

____

____

____

THE 50 COFFEE ADVENTURE NUMBER (25)

Date and time: **Location:**

Person:

What did I learn from the experience of having this coffee?

How has it changed the way I see the world?

How will it change the way I move forward?

What can I learn from this, to impact my mission?

Was there anything that triggered discomfort in this conversation? And why?

What commitments did I make, that I need to act on?

How could I improve the way I have coffee?

Are there any other people I need to have coffee with, as a result of this conversation?

THE 50 COFFEE ADVENTURE NUMBER (26)

Date and time: **Location:**

Person:

What did I learn from the experience of having this coffee?

How has it changed the way I see the world?

How will it change the way I move forward?

What can I learn from this, to impact my mission?

Was there anything that triggered discomfort in this conversation? And why?

What commitments did I make, that I need to act on?

How could I improve the way I have coffee?

Are there any other people I need to have coffee with, as a result of this conversation?

THE 50 COFFEE ADVENTURE NUMBER (27)

Date and time: ________________________   **Location:** ________________

Person: ____

What did I learn from the experience of having this coffee? ________________
____

How has it changed the way I see the world? ______________________________
____

How will it change the way I move forward? _______________________________
____

What can I learn from this, to impact my mission? _________________________
____

Was there anything that triggered discomfort in this conversation? And why? __
____

What commitments did I make, that I need to act on? ______________________
____

How could I improve the way I have coffee? _______________________________
____

Are there any other people I need to have coffee with, as a result of this conversation?
____
____
____
____

THE 50 COFFEE ADVENTURE NUMBER (28)

Date and time: **Location:**

Person:

What did I learn from the experience of having this coffee?

How has it changed the way I see the world?

How will it change the way I move forward?

What can I learn from this, to impact my mission?

Was there anything that triggered discomfort in this conversation? And why?

What commitments did I make, that I need to act on?

How could I improve the way I have coffee?

Are there any other people I need to have coffee with, as a result of this conversation?

THE 50 COFFEE ADVENTURE NUMBER (29)

Date and time: ___________________   **Location:** ___________________

Person: ___________________

What did I learn from the experience of having this coffee? ___________________

____

How has it changed the way I see the world? ___________________

____

How will it change the way I move forward? ___________________

____

What can I learn from this, to impact my mission? ___________________

____

Was there anything that triggered discomfort in this conversation? And why? ___________________

____

What commitments did I make, that I need to act on? ___________________

____

How could I improve the way I have coffee? ___________________

____

Are there any other people I need to have coffee with, as a result of this conversation?

____

____

____

THE 50 COFFEE ADVENTURE NUMBER  30

Date and time: **Location:**

Person:

What did I learn from the experience of having this coffee?

How has it changed the way I see the world?

How will it change the way I move forward?

What can I learn from this, to impact my mission?

Was there anything that triggered discomfort in this conversation? And why?

What commitments did I make, that I need to act on?

How could I improve the way I have coffee?

Are there any other people I need to have coffee with, as a result of this conversation?

THE 50 COFFEE ADVENTURE NUMBER (31)

Date and time: _______________________   **Location:** _______________________

Person: _______________________

What did I learn from the experience of having this coffee?

____

How has it changed the way I see the world?

____

How will it change the way I move forward?

____

What can I learn from this, to impact my mission?

____

Was there anything that triggered discomfort in this conversation? And why?

____

What commitments did I make, that I need to act on?

____

How could I improve the way I have coffee?

____

Are there any other people I need to have coffee with, as a result of this conversation?

____

____

____

THE 50 COFFEE ADVENTURE NUMBER 

Date and time: **Location:**

Person:

What did I learn from the experience of having this coffee?

How has it changed the way I see the world?

How will it change the way I move forward?

What can I learn from this, to impact my mission?

Was there anything that triggered discomfort in this conversation? And why?

What commitments did I make, that I need to act on?

How could I improve the way I have coffee?

Are there any other people I need to have coffee with, as a result of this conversation?

THE 50 COFFEE ADVENTURE NUMBER (33)

Date and time: **Location:**

Person:

What did I learn from the experience of having this coffee?

How has it changed the way I see the world?

How will it change the way I move forward?

What can I learn from this, to impact my mission?

Was there anything that triggered discomfort in this conversation? And why?

What commitments did I make, that I need to act on?

How could I improve the way I have coffee?

Are there any other people I need to have coffee with, as a result of this conversation?

THE 50 COFFEE ADVENTURE NUMBER  **34**

Date and time: ___________________________ **Location:** _______________________

Person: ____

What did I learn from the experience of having this coffee? _______________________

____

How has it changed the way I see the world? _____________________________________

____

How will it change the way I move forward? ______________________________________

____

What can I learn from this, to impact my mission? ________________________________

____

Was there anything that triggered discomfort in this conversation? And why? _________

____

What commitments did I make, that I need to act on? ______________________________

____

How could I improve the way I have coffee? ______________________________________

____

Are there any other people I need to have coffee with, as a result of this conversation?

____

____

____

THE 50 COFFEE ADVENTURE NUMBER  35

Date and time: **Location:**

Person:

What did I learn from the experience of having this coffee?

How has it changed the way I see the world?

How will it change the way I move forward?

What can I learn from this, to impact my mission?

Was there anything that triggered discomfort in this conversation? And why?

What commitments did I make, that I need to act on?

How could I improve the way I have coffee?

Are there any other people I need to have coffee with, as a result of this conversation?

THE 50 COFFEE ADVENTURE NUMBER  36

Date and time: **Location:**

Person:

What did I learn from the experience of having this coffee?

How has it changed the way I see the world?

How will it change the way I move forward?

What can I learn from this, to impact my mission?

Was there anything that triggered discomfort in this conversation? And why?

What commitments did I make, that I need to act on?

How could I improve the way I have coffee?

Are there any other people I need to have coffee with, as a result of this conversation?

THE 50 COFFEE ADVENTURE NUMBER  37

Date and time: **Location:**

Person:

What did I learn from the experience of having this coffee?

How has it changed the way I see the world?

How will it change the way I move forward?

What can I learn from this, to impact my mission?

Was there anything that triggered discomfort in this conversation? And why?

What commitments did I make, that I need to act on?

How could I improve the way I have coffee?

Are there any other people I need to have coffee with, as a result of this conversation?

THE 50 COFFEE ADVENTURE NUMBER 38

Date and time: ________________________ **Location:** ________________________

Person: ____

What did I learn from the experience of having this coffee? ______________________

____

How has it changed the way I see the world? __________________________________

____

How will it change the way I move forward? __________________________________

____

What can I learn from this, to impact my mission? ______________________________

____

Was there anything that triggered discomfort in this conversation? And why? ________

____

What commitments did I make, that I need to act on? ____________________________

____

How could I improve the way I have coffee? __________________________________

____

Are there any other people I need to have coffee with, as a result of this conversation?

____

____

____

THE 50 COFFEE ADVENTURE NUMBER  39

Date and time: _______________________   **Location:** _______________________

Person: ____

What did I learn from the experience of having this coffee? _________________

____

How has it changed the way I see the world? ______________________________

____

How will it change the way I move forward? _______________________________

____

____

What can I learn from this, to impact my mission? _________________________

____

Was there anything that triggered discomfort in this conversation? And why? ___

____

What commitments did I make, that I need to act on? ______________________

____

How could I improve the way I have coffee? ______________________________

____

Are there any other people I need to have coffee with, as a result of this conversation?

____

____

____

THE 50 COFFEE ADVENTURE NUMBER (40)

Date and time: ___________________________ **Location:** ___________________________

Person: ____

What did I learn from the experience of having this coffee? ___________________________

____

How has it changed the way I see the world? ___________________________________

____

How will it change the way I move forward? ___________________________________

____

What can I learn from this, to impact my mission? ___________________________

____

Was there anything that triggered discomfort in this conversation? And why? _________

____

What commitments did I make, that I need to act on? ___________________________

____

How could I improve the way I have coffee? ___________________________________

____

Are there any other people I need to have coffee with, as a result of this conversation?

____

____

THE 50 COFFEE ADVENTURE NUMBER (41)

Date and time: **Location:**

Person:

What did I learn from the experience of having this coffee?

How has it changed the way I see the world?

How will it change the way I move forward?

What can I learn from this, to impact my mission?

Was there anything that triggered discomfort in this conversation? And why?

What commitments did I make, that I need to act on?

How could I improve the way I have coffee?

Are there any other people I need to have coffee with, as a result of this conversation?

THE 50 COFFEE ADVENTURE NUMBER  42

Date and time: ____________________ **Location:** ____________________

Person: ____________________

What did I learn from the experience of having this coffee? ____________

____

How has it changed the way I see the world? ____________________

____

How will it change the way I move forward? ____________________

____

What can I learn from this, to impact my mission? ____________________

____

Was there anything that triggered discomfort in this conversation? And why? ______

____

What commitments did I make, that I need to act on? ____________________

____

How could I improve the way I have coffee? ____________________

____

Are there any other people I need to have coffee with, as a result of this conversation?

____

____

THE 50 COFFEE ADVENTURE NUMBER  43

Date and time: ___________________________   **Location:** ___________________________

Person: ____

What did I learn from the experience of having this coffee?

____

How has it changed the way I see the world?

____

How will it change the way I move forward?

____

What can I learn from this, to impact my mission?

____

Was there anything that triggered discomfort in this conversation? And why?

____

What commitments did I make, that I need to act on?

____

How could I improve the way I have coffee?

____

Are there any other people I need to have coffee with, as a result of this conversation?

____

____

____

THE 50 COFFEE ADVENTURE NUMBER  44

Date and time: **Location:**

Person:

What did I learn from the experience of having this coffee?

How has it changed the way I see the world?

How will it change the way I move forward?

What can I learn from this, to impact my mission?

Was there anything that triggered discomfort in this conversation? And why?

What commitments did I make, that I need to act on?

How could I improve the way I have coffee?

Are there any other people I need to have coffee with, as a result of this conversation?

THE 50 COFFEE ADVENTURE NUMBER  45

Date and time: ____________________ **Location:** ____________________

Person: ____________________

What did I learn from the experience of having this coffee?

____

How has it changed the way I see the world?

____

How will it change the way I move forward?

____

What can I learn from this, to impact my mission?

____

Was there anything that triggered discomfort in this conversation? And why?

____

What commitments did I make, that I need to act on?

____

How could I improve the way I have coffee?

____

Are there any other people I need to have coffee with, as a result of this conversation?

____

____

____

THE 50 COFFEE ADVENTURE NUMBER  **46**

Date and time: **Location:**

Person:

What did I learn from the experience of having this coffee?

How has it changed the way I see the world?

How will it change the way I move forward?

What can I learn from this, to impact my mission?

Was there anything that triggered discomfort in this conversation? And why?

What commitments did I make, that I need to act on?

How could I improve the way I have coffee?

Are there any other people I need to have coffee with, as a result of this conversation?

THE 50 COFFEE ADVENTURE NUMBER (47)

Date and time: **Location:**

Person:

What did I learn from the experience of having this coffee?

How has it changed the way I see the world?

How will it change the way I move forward?

What can I learn from this, to impact my mission?

Was there anything that triggered discomfort in this conversation? And why?

What commitments did I make, that I need to act on?

How could I improve the way I have coffee?

Are there any other people I need to have coffee with, as a result of this conversation?

THE 50 COFFEE ADVENTURE NUMBER  48

Date and time: _______________________ **Location:** _______________________

Person: ____

What did I learn from the experience of having this coffee? _______________

____

How has it changed the way I see the world? _____________________________

____

How will it change the way I move forward? ______________________________

____

What can I learn from this, to impact my mission? ________________________

____

Was there anything that triggered discomfort in this conversation? And why? __

____

What commitments did I make, that I need to act on? ______________________

____

How could I improve the way I have coffee? _____________________________

____

Are there any other people I need to have coffee with, as a result of this conversation?

____

____

____

THE 50 COFFEE ADVENTURE NUMBER  49

Date and time: **Location:**

Person:

What did I learn from the experience of having this coffee?

How has it changed the way I see the world?

How will it change the way I move forward?

What can I learn from this, to impact my mission?

Was there anything that triggered discomfort in this conversation? And why?

What commitments did I make, that I need to act on?

How could I improve the way I have coffee?

Are there any other people I need to have coffee with, as a result of this conversation?

THE 50 COFFEE ADVENTURE NUMBER  50

Date and time: ________________________ **Location:** ________________

Person: ____

What did I learn from the experience of having this coffee? _________________

____

How has it changed the way I see the world? ______________________________

____

How will it change the way I move forward? ______________________________

____

What can I learn from this, to impact my mission? _________________________

____

Was there anything that triggered discomfort in this conversation? And why? ____

____

What commitments did I make, that I need to act on? ______________________

____

How could I improve the way I have coffee? ______________________________

____

Are there any other people I need to have coffee with, as a result of this conversation?

____

____

Reflections and actions

Please understand that it's much easier than you think to make changes, and there's always something to learn about the power of human connection. Whether you have actively taken part in the whole challenge or only read the recipes at this stage, it's important to reflect on how it has changed you. Revisit this section after you've had 20, 30, or 50 coffees. Notice what's changed. No matter how subtle or small, a change for the better makes a real difference – and causes a ripple effect.

To maximise the effects, take the time to consciously reflect on this experience. Think about how it has changed you, now. And consider its capacity to change you and those around you in the long term.

Take a few deep breaths and ask yourself the following questions about this experience:

Which aspect/s would you like to continue and make permanent, in your life?

How can you implement them into your normal day-to-day routine?

What is the least you can change, to make the biggest difference?

If there was one simple thing you could change – what would it be?

In what way(s) do you feel empowered to change the world?

How has this experience changed your life?

How will this experience change the world?

Share your story about this experience with your friends and network. Hopefully, it will inspire others to take on a similar adventure and gain positive learning experiences of their own.

Remember to use #50coffees if you're sharing on social media. We would love to hear your story too. Send us your 50 Coffee Adventure story to yourstory@50coffees.org and let us know if you are happy for us to publish to the 50 Coffee Adventure community and the 50 Coffee Adventure Facebook group.

If you have any feedback on the 50 Coffee Adventure, or you think it can be improved in any way, please get in touch at feedback@50coffees.org.

50 great questions to ask in a Coffee

1. What's important to you, in life?
2. If you could improve the world by doing one thing, what would you choose to do?
3. If you could go back in time, what's one piece of advice you'd give to your younger self?
4. What's most important to you about the work you do?
5. What's the biggest challenge or struggle you've ever faced?
6. Tell me your story.
7. If you died today, is there something you would regret not doing or saying?
8. If you had $100,000 to give away to any cause, what would you choose, and why?
9. What are you most grateful for in, your life?
10. If you had a chance to design your life from scratch – would you build it this way again?
11. What aspects of your life would you change, and why?
12. If you started again from a blank sheet, how would you build your life?
13. What do you think are the five most important traits for a person to have?
14. In which situations do you feel most comfortable sharing your perspective?
15. Tell me about your health and wellbeing.
16. Is there something you've dreamed of doing for a long time? Why haven't you done it yet?
17. Who is your hero and what qualities do they have, that you admire?
18. If you only had one year left to live, would you change anything about the way you are now living? Why?
19. Who do you trust? And why?
20. What is your biggest challenge or struggle, at the moment?
21. What makes you happy?
22. Have you ever had the opportunity to help someone? Tell me about it.
23. Tell me what motivates you.
24. What do you think you will be doing ten years from now?
25. Has someone ever really helped you? Tell me about it.
26. What are your greatest weaknesses?
27. Tell me about your hopes.
28. What's the best advice you've been given?
29. If you had a million dollars to spare, what would you do?
30. Tell me your life story in four minutes, with as many details as possible.

31. What are your greatest strengths?
32. Tell me three things that happened in the last week, that you're thankful for.
33. What do you value most in your life?
34. What is your major goal in life?
35. How do you best connect with others?
36. What are the three most important things on your bucket list?
37. What are your favourite three topics to talk about?
38. Tell me about a day you had that you'll never forget.
39. What controversial issue – social or political – do you feel strongly about? Why?
40. What is the best thing that's ever happened to you?
41. What do you value most in a friendship?
42. What are your biggest goals for this year? How will you work to achieve them?
43. What would you like people to say about you after you die?
44. What's something you want to do in the next year that you've never done before?
45. What would constitute a "perfect" day for you?
46. What is the most frightening thing you have ever done?
47. Whom do you respect? Why?
48. If you could have three wishes, what would you wish for?
49. If you could take a year-long paid sabbatical, what would you do?
50. If your family and friends were asked to describe you, who would provide the most accurate description? What do you think they would say?

The author and the backstory

My name is Marc Winn and I am on a mission to change the world, one coffee at a time. This book is based on action research over nearly a decade, which took the form of meeting people for coffee and using this as a vehicle to transform my life – and the life of others. After seeing the transformational power of coffee on myself, and on my local and global community, and after building connections and finding solutions to important issues – I wanted to share this.

My story

I grew up in an entrepreneurial family, in which the dining room table was the boardroom table. From birth, I was exposed to unconventional experiences around the world that helped to develop a highly questioning mind with a fascination for seeing how things worked and related to each other.

From early on, not much of the world seemed to make sense to me. Two big things sold to everyone is 'make money' and 'get a good education'. My Dad always made a lot of money, yet he'd left school at 14 with little education. He was always more successful than most people, yet I'd openly question that his wealth brought him true fulfilment, for a significant part of his life. I spent time growing up in Africa and witnessed more joy on the faces of people with nothing than I ever witnessed in places where resources are abundant.

Since school, I was consistently 'measured' with the phrase 'has potential, but must try harder'. I was seen as highly gifted but very lazy. In reality, I couldn't motivate myself to buy into a world I just didn't believe in, at its root. It was all part of a 30-year battle to get out of bed in the morning. If I'd visited a doctor, I would most likely have received a significant mental health diagnosis and been taking pills for the rest of my life.

By the time I was 32, I had GCSEs, A-Levels, two degrees, and I'd built and sold an eight-figure direct marketing business with my brother. All without much motivation and never truly loving what I did. Without working that hard, too.

I developed two hyper skills in that time. The first was how to find the shortest route to do something, and the second was the ability to manipulate other people to do things for me. I'm as good as it gets in both of these skills. I remained fascinated by contrarian thinking and obsessed with outliers who chose to do things differently – and I longed to be allowed to live that way.

I didn't enjoy work and education much, because what really inspired me wasn't at the core of traditional education or business.

I would describe myself as 'highly misunderstood' during those years. Not able to properly express the things I could see and feel; screaming inside a glass box that I couldn't get out of. I could see things that others couldn't, although I had no idea how or why. The loneliness was so deep and the yearning to truly connect with others was, at times, overwhelming. Being so sure in your own mind – while the whole world treats you as if you've lost it – was highly damaging, over time. During my entrepreneurial career, I had two nervous breakdowns, caused by not being true to who I was.

My joys were brief and hedonistic: drinking, eating, travel and watching sport. I would pursue peak experiences to try to feel good at some level. The rest of the time, I felt numb and disengaged... just doing what had to be done.

My life changed in 2008, when I started mentoring entrepreneurs. I was hooked. I had all the joy and interest of working with people on interesting things – yet I didn't have to do any of the work! I briefly and unsuccessfully tried investing, but soon realised that I wasn't really interested in the returns – I was more interested in helping people to thrive. I became really good at helping entrepreneurs with strategies for building businesses aligned with who they really are. Moving them from being slaves to business, to developing businesses that served their highest values and purpose. I was training people to become free-thinking linky brains. I also became very good at getting people to leave their jobs.

In 2010, I had an epiphany of self-forgiveness whilst reading Tim Ferris's book *The 4-Hour Work Week*. I'd come across a way to use my two hyper skills to make a difference to millions of lives, at scale! It took me six months to get off the ceiling, while I restructured all of my life and personal branding around who I truly was. During that time, I finally accepted myself and began to move from self-hatred to self-love. I was going to be the guy who did the least to achieve the most. I was going to be the person who took leverage to a whole new level.

The big mission

During a conversation with a friend, in which I confessed that I wanted to change the world, I was given a lead – to visit a cutting-edge technology institution that trains people to change the world! As a result, in 2013, I went to Silicon Valley and attended Singularity University, founded by Ray Kurzweil (Director of Engineering at Google) and

Peter Diamandis (Founder of the XPrize). The mission of SU is to solve the world's grand challenges through the use of technology. Participants are encouraged to work on a project that will positively impact a billion lives within 10 years.

During my time there, I realised there was a strong need and role in the world for 'connectors' as well as doers. As a result, I set my own personal mission to positively impact a billion people – just by having coffee.

Whilst I loved what I'd learnt, I also saw people recreating the same problems I had already seen and experienced. Entrepreneurs building and growing organisations by following sets of pre-defined cultural rules, rather than shaping those organisations and missions around what was best for the entrepreneur.

I announced publicly that I was going to positively impact a billion people within 10 years. My mission was to do all that by just having coffee.

I also realised that people spoke about government as though it was an unsolvable problem. Growing up and living in Guernsey – a 'tax haven' – I saw people change legislation and policy to create wealth. I quickly joined the dots: those same mechanisms could be used to make it easier to do new things in healthcare, education, welfare etc.

During a coffee in 2013, I co-founded and launched a moonshot project, named the Dandelion Project, which aimed to use a small self-governing nation state to solve all the world's major systemic issues. We set a mission to make Guernsey the best place to live on earth by 2020. Guernsey is a self-governing nation of 25 square miles with a population of 63,000. There, you can solve major issues at coffee scale. This dynamic turns impossible problems into problems that are just possible to solve.

As part of this ambitious project, we developed our 'coffee for Impact' programme, in which we have coffee with changemakers and encourage other people in our community to have coffee to solve problems. This book is a product of the work and research on this mission.

Guernsey is the birthplace of a new kind of systemic revolution of grassroots problem-solving never witnessed before. A system that has been unlocked coffee by coffee, event by event, to empower people to find their true potential. We now have a collective of individual hearts and minds within a small place, with both the desire and the power to change things relatively quickly.

Ironically, the project I work on now is not the most impactful thing I have done. The highest impact I've had to date was from spending 45 mins on a blog post. This created a worldwide meme seen by tens of millions of people, transforming countless lives. It was the ultimate act of dot-joining – bringing together a venn diagram around purpose with the Japanese concept of Ikigai. It just got out of hand.

The really important stuff

I have three beautiful children: Charlie, Bertie and Emilie. I married a highly talented change-maker called Valerie, who is working on transforming education, amongst other things. I could happily die tomorrow, thankful that I found my way out of the cage and connected with who I really am. There was a long time when that wasn't the case. Now, I'm truly happy.

More information about me http://www.marcwinn.com

Acknowledgements

There are so many people I have to thank. This book is the sum of all of my experiences, crystalised into one journey. I would find it impossible to remember and thank everyone who was involved in this project in some way.

To the Happy (Bern) Lab, where this project was conceived and initially funded.

To my editor, Linda Innes, who turns my ideas into something readable. There are many of her great ideas in this, too.

To my wonderful assistant, Jayne Packer, who helped me along most of my adventure in making impact with coffee.

To Sachin Patel, who inspired me to turn this from a book into an adventure. To Tim Ferris, for inspiring me to make less more.

To all the guys at Singularity University, for making me believe that I can change the world.

To Chris Bader, (the first guy I ever mentored), for getting me into coffee. To John Sweeney, for teaching me how small actions and coffee can make a ding in the universe.

To all the people who provided feedback to improve this challenge. In particular, Mike Baxter and Sunny Sangha.

To all the thousands of people I've had coffee with, over the years. I couldn't have done it without you.

To my incredible home community of Guernsey that inspires me every day.

To Eileen and the Get Up and Go Publications team for making this a reality.

To my Dad, who without doubt, is the greatest influence and inspiration in my life. To my Mum, who – despite how challenging I was – loved me with all her heart. To my brother, Graham, who worked far harder than me in the first part of my entrepreneurial journey.

To Jock, who was stupid enough to say yes to my crazy plan to change the world. You are my hero.

To my kids, for making me want to be a better person and leave a better world. To my wonderful wife, Valerie, who was always covering for me whilst I was out having coffee. You inspire me more than you will ever know.

To you. Thank you for showing up in my life.

Marc Winn

Made in the USA
Las Vegas, NV
02 January 2022